Public Access Microcomputers

A Handbook for Librarians

by Patrick R. Dewey

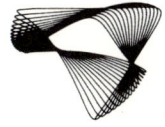

Knowledge Industry Publications, Inc.

White Plains, NY and London

Professional Librarian Series

Public Access Microcomputers: A Handbook for Librarians

Library of Congress Cataloging in Publication Data

Dewey, Patrick R., 1949
    Public access microcomputers.

    (Professional librarian series)
    Bibliography: p.
    Includes index.
    1. Information storage and retrieval systems.
2. Microcomputers—Library applications. 3. On-line bibliographic searching. 4. Libraries—Automation.
5. Library science—Data processing. I. Title.
II. Series.
Z699.D47   1984   025'.04   83-26776
ISBN 0-86729-086-2
ISBN 0-86729-085-4 (soft)

Printed in the United States of America

Copyright © 1984 by Knowledge Industry Publications, Inc., 701 Westchester Ave., White Plains, NY 10604. Not to be reproduced in any form whatever without written permission from the publisher.

10   9   8   7   6   5   4   3   2   1

Table of Contents

List of Tables and Figures iv
List of Photographs iv
Preface 1
1. Getting Started 3
2. Choosing the Micro That Meets Your Needs 15
3. Choosing and Evaluating Software 29
4. Managing the Project 51
5. Examples of Public Access Projects 67
6. Clubs, Special Events and Other Activities 87
7. Electronic Bulletin Boards and Other Data Base Services 103
Afterword: The Future of Public Access Microcomputers 123
Appendix A: Friends of the Chicago Public Library—Grant Proposal .. 125
Appendix B: Manufacturers of Microcomputers Used in Public Access
    Programs 128
Appendix C: Selected Software Companies 129
Appendix D: Selected Coinop Companies 132
Appendix E: Microcomputer Newsletters and Journals 132
Appendix F: Bulletin Board Software Sources 134
Glossary 135
Selected Bibliography 139
Index 147
About the Author 151

List of Tables and Figures

Table 2.1: Comparison of Micro Equipment and Capabilities 18

Table 3.1: North-Pulaski Computer Use, May 1983 30
Figure 3.1: North Pulaski Software Review Form 39
Figure 3.2: Portion of North-Pulaski Software Wall Chart 46

Figure 4.1: North-Pulaski Computer Center Appointment Slip 61
Figure 4.2: North Pulaski User Agreement 61

Table 5.1: Comparison of Library Public Access Projects 68
Figure 5.1: Downers Grove Public Access Press Release 76
Figure 5.2: Frankfort Public Library Microcomputer Guidelines 77
Figure 5.3: Rolling Meadows Library Computer Rules 82
Figure 5.4: Rolling Meadows Library Apple Computer Worksheet 83

Figure 6.1: Library Microcomputer Users Application Form 91
Figure 6.2: North-Pulaski Exit Survey 98
Figure 6.3: Follow-up Publicity Announcement 98
Figure 6.4: North-Pulaski Promotional Flier 100

Figure 7.1: Opening Message Display 106
Figure 7.2: Partial Message Scan 107
Figure 7.3: Sample Message 108
Figure 7.4: Feature Articles Display 109
Figure 7.5: Download Instructions on the North-Pulaski BBS 110
Figure 7.6: North-Pulaski Log File Display 113
Figure 7.7: North-Pulaski BBS Censorship Message 114
Table 7.1: Comparison of Online Consumer Networks 118
Figure 7.8: Sample entries from Subject Guide Wall Chart 121

List of Photographs

The CompuVend coinop micro workstation 27
The Anchor Pad computer system 53
A young patron at the North-Pulaski personal computer center 72
Pascal Place at the Liverpool Public Library 78
Word processing seminar at the North-Pulaski Branch Library 96
The Computer News Center bulletin board at North-Pulaski 101
A young patron consults the Subject Guide Wall Chart 120

ACKNOWLEDGMENTS

There are many more people who helped me with this book than I can thank individually. Those most prominent in my mind include: Marvin Garber, whose tremendous day-to-day attention to details at the Personal Computer Center has given me so much to write about; Roberta Petz, Northwest district chief, whose enthusiasm for libraries I have always appreciated; Peggy Sullivan, who helped to nudge me in the right direction; Mildred Vannorsdall, librarian of the Professional Library of the Chicago Public Library; the staff of the North-Pulaski Branch Library; the many librarians involved with the public access projects described herein; and the Friends of the Chicago Public Library, who have been friends indeed.

This book is for my parents:
Hazel and Joseph Dewey
and for
Don, Barb, Erin
and, not to be forgotten,
Tinkerbelle

Preface

Oh good grief, another book on microcomputers!

The microcomputer world is vast, involving millions of people and billions of dollars. It seems to have sprung up overnight and now touches nearly every aspect of life, including home, school, business and entertainment. A casual perusal of book and magazine stands reveals numerous microcomputer titles covering many and varied aspects of the world of microcomputers. This book is about a very small and specific—but important—corner of that world.

Two years of public access efforts by the staff of the North-Pulaski Branch of the Chicago Public Library have been fruitful and exciting. They have not been easy. After years of largely unsuccessful attempts to get patrons to show up at every imaginable inner city program, few of us were really ready when everyone decided to show up for the microcomputer. It seems that the time is just right for libraries to make the most of a tremendous promotional tool: public access microcomputers.

Anyone observing libraries with such services is immediately struck by the individuality of each library's program. They all do it differently, reflecting the versatility of the microcomputer. A major goal of this book is to inspire ideas and encourage readers to experiment. The book is also intended to help them avoid many of the initial pitfalls and problems in the process.

This is not a book about the many administrative or internal uses to which a microcomputer can obviously be put, such as catalog card and overdue notice production or circulation control. Further, no effort will be made to give anyone a quick course in microelectronics or computer science, both of which are beyond the scope of this book. We will only touch upon the essential aspects of hardware necessary for the introduction of public access microcomputers into the library.

Advice in Chapters 1 through 4 centers around the "basic three": identification of community and library needs and the corresponding level of service required; the selection and purchase of hardware and software to fill those needs; and the control and management of what is ultimately acquired.

In Chapter 5, examples of public access projects in a number of libraries around the country provide a look at the many activities typical to personal computer centers. These should serve as helpful sources for ideas and suggestions, saving the beginner a great deal of time. The primary mission and concerns of managing a small- to medium-sized library will not be neglected: How does this technology fit in with the delivery of other library services? Can the potential impact of an increased workload be minimized?

Special activities, events and library computer clubs are discussed in Chapter 6, along with ways to promote these and other services. In Chapter 7, we will consider the newest and perhaps most exciting areas of service: public access to library-produced and remote data bases, and patron access to the library electronic bulletin board from home.

Examples of software are sprinkled throughout the book, many for the Apple computer—since that is where the bulk of my experience lies—but for other computers as well. Readers should keep in mind that these are presented only as examples and are not meant to be a comprehensive list. Do not select software here; look in the manner described and in the sources listed.

Finally, there are many more micros, types of software and peripherals that are on the market—or will be by the time this book is published—than we have described here. This book reports on those systems that have been used and tested in library public access programs to date. Other systems may work well for public access, so by all means investigate thoroughly before you purchase, and select the system that best suits your library's needs and the community it serves.

Patrick R. Dewey
February 1984

1

Getting Started

WHAT ARE PUBLIC ACCESS MICROCOMPUTERS?

The concept of "public access microcomputers" refers to any microcomputer-based service directly available for public use, usually in a public library. It should be distinguished from "public access computers," which might pertain to any sort of computer, including mainframes.[1] This definition of public access microcomputers encompasses many different levels of services. It includes "hands-on" use of the equipment by patrons; using a micro to produce reference materials, such as wall charts; operating a community electronic bulletin board system (BBS); and providing online access to library-produced files and to other data base systems.

Public access micros were probably first installed in a public library in 1977.[2] They had small 8K memories and were not capable of many of the above projects. Even with their deficiencies, early public access micros were an immediate hit. As more complete and sophisticated systems (with disk drives, printers and modems) were installed, enthusiastic librarians began reporting almost universal success. It became evident that the public's curiosity about microcomputers was boundless.

In 1979 the ComputerTown USA! project was started. Four micros installed in the Menlo Park (CA) Public Library, the original ComputerTown, brought enthusiastic response from the community. (ComputerTown USA! is discussed more fully in Chapter 5.)

By 1981 some libraries had set up "computer centers" and "computer rooms," and others began workshops for patron training and "computer reading clubs" for children. A survey conducted in April 1982 by Kusack and Bowers, to determine the level of public access service in libraries, revealed the "drawing power of the microcomputer." One librarian reported "traffic jams," while another said that "the Adult Continuing Education Department has experienced a 40% increase in the number of patrons [who] use the department."[3]

"Coinop" companies eventually appeared on the scene, and the first library microcomputer electronic bulletin board system for the public was established in late 1981.[4] Computer or software "fairs" (see Chapter 6) began popping up, even in libraries without public computers, and a few libraries began circulating small microcomputers such as the Sinclair ZX81. At least one library began making the Texas Instruments Speak N' Spell unit available to patrons.

Examples of innovative uses of micros in libraries have proliferated. A library in California created a computer van that takes 15 microcomputers on classroom visits. Some 8000 children have enjoyed this approach.[5] Elsewhere, a few experiments with online microcomputer services through consumer networks such as The Source and CompuServe have also been attempted. Some school and academic libraries began offering online encyclopedias to students in 1983.[6]

By late 1982, recognizing the need to share their knowledge, librarians in several states had organized into user groups, and several public access conferences were held.

THE PURPOSE OF PUBLIC ACCESS

Most librarians would probably agree that part of the public access microcomputer effort is aimed at providing the local community with "computer literacy"; the rest is part of the age-old library tradition of providing information and recreation. Beverly Hunter supplied a practical, broad-based definition of computer literacy in 1981:

> Computer literacy is whatever a person needs to be able to know about and do with computers in order to function effectively in our information-based society. This definition points out that what skills and knowledges and attitudes are needed will vary from person to person and from time to time, depending on what it is they are doing. This definition also points out that computers are tools in service of other work—not an end in themselves.[7]

Most of the people using a public microcomputer will be *non-librarians*, doing non-library chores. Micro use will fall into the broad categories of education, entertainment and practical functions, such as word processing, data base management, etc. Specific uses would fill an encyclopedia.

All age groups will find some use for the machine and all will have a natural curiosity about what it will do and how it might help them in life. Statistics from the North-Pulaski Branch Library (of the Chicago Public Library) show that in 1982 approximately 14% of all public access micro users were under the age of 12, 46% were from 12 to 21, and 40% were over 21. Preschoolers and senior citizens registered approximately 1% each.[8]

The most obvious benefit of a public access micro program is that it gives those who don't have access to micros—or are hesitant about tackling a new technology—the chance to try them. Statistics reported for the first six months of microcomputer use at the Forsyth County (NC) Public Library indicate that ". . . over 40% of users had no previous experience and that most, at least initially, wanted computer skills (i.e., to know how micros work)."[9]

For many in the community, a public access micro may represent the best opportunity to gain experience with a computer. People want to see it, touch it and "kick the tires." Small businesses want the same try-out privileges. Students will also make use of library microcomputers. Although a recent study shows that more than two-thirds of all public schools have at least one microcomputer, not every student will have the chance to use one.[10]

Children are especially attracted to the micro. We are told that they will be living and growing with computers at home, school and work from now on. In some cases, public access micros are the only way a child can get close to a computer.

A public access microcomputer also benefits those who already have (or have access to) microcomputers. Library software collections are useful in the same way as book collections: Few people can afford to buy all the books that they wish to read. Until these needs subside, the library—especially the public library—is clearly the only place where many people can go for hands-on experience.

CHOOSING AREAS OF SERVICE

The first question for libraries to consider is: Is a personal computer center needed or possible? Not every library can or should have microcomputer service. It's important to remember that libraries, like people, are all different and each must fix the level of public access best managed and justified by the available staff and resources. Service can be simple or complex, superficial or comprehensive. Some general levels of public access service are listed below. All are discussed in the chapters to follow.

1. *No service*: Some small libraries may be physically unable to accommodate the many additional people a micro attracts. Security and other factors may also play a part in determining if a microcomputer should be installed.

2. *Moderate equipment and software*: This level may be as simple as providing Speak N' Spell. Computers with little software, small memories and no disk drives are the usual fare.

3. *Full service*: This means providing extensive software and/or hardware, including disk drives and a printer.

4. *Library-sponsored activities*: This level of service includes library-sponsored computer classes or computer clubs, in addition to equipment and software.

5. *Online services*: By means of a telecommunications link, libraries can provide the community with online services, such as the electronic bulletin board system, or access to networks such as The Source or CompuServe.

6. *Loan of software or hardware*: Some libraries may wish to circulate hardware or software to patrons. In the case of software circulation, libraries must make provisions for patrons to copy the programs they wish to borrow. For this reason, only public domain software can be considered for a software loan program. Libraries that lend equipment usually choose inexpensive machines for this purpose (see Chapter 4).

7. *Help (tutoring)*: Generally, this area is for academic and school libraries, since most public libraries cannot invest the time and staff necessary for such service.

8. *Software fairs, festivals, etc.*: These can be organized on a one-time basis (for libraries unable to provide other levels of service) or as ongoing events.

9. *Computer-assisted instruction (CAI)*: A library usually undertakes a CAI program as a cooperative effort with a school or in conjunction with in-house classes.

10. *Software collection*: This constitutes a multitude of levels, from elementary BASIC through more sophisticated programs.

11. *Library-produced data bases*: These include electronic bulletin board systems, wall charts for patron reference and any other library-produced data bases for public access.

It is impossible to delineate these areas exactly and many levels overlap, even in the same library or library system. They do not follow in a neat ladder format: e.g., it is not necessary for a library to offer full service for it to sponsor activities. The natural progression of adding equipment in response to patron demand may lead from one level to another. Each library will determine the level of service based on its own resources and on community needs (see Chapter 2). Some guidelines for getting started follow.

WHERE DO WE START?

Professional library staff time devoted to a micro project should not be excessive. Even so, learning about and using microcomputer equipment and software takes time and is the only sure way to have a successful program. Do not be a stranger to the equipment: Start with yourself.

Before purchasing, or before considering any particular microcomputer for purchase, browse through microcomputer journals and magazines. Attend local workshops, conferences, training sessions or software fairs. Visit a local library where such equipment is already in use and ask questions. If you have access to a micro on a regular basis, work with programs as often as possible. Start with simple ones and work up. Don't expect miracles overnight, but you should see some real progress in just a few weeks. Do not enroll in a programming course immediately; that can always be done later.

Experimenting with micros and various types of software is the best way to understand what a micro can do. However, before you can make any decisions about which micro to buy or which software to select, you must become familiar with basic micro hardware and software terminology.

LEARNING THE VOCABULARY

Since small computers are fundamentally not much different from their big brothers, most of what librarians already know of computer components will be directly applicable to micros. The terms "personal," "home" and "desk-top" computer are used fairly interchangeably with the word "microcomputer."

Hardware and Software

For convenience, we will begin our discussion by dividing the computer operation (aside from the human element) into two parts: *hardware* and *software*. Hardware includes all metal and plastic components, and silicon chips, that can be touched and picked up (and broken!). Software includes the *programs* and *data* that give the computer its individual capabilities and versatility. Programs and data change very rapidly; the hardware, very slowly. Programs can be roughly divided further into *applications software* and *systems software*. Applications software includes programs of major interest to the end user (whoever is using the micro). Within this category are games, educational programs, business programs, etc. Systems software refers to all programs that enable a computer to function and control its own operations. It includes, among other things, the operating system, assemblers and compilers. This book will concern itself mainly with applications software, the subject of Chapter 3.

Input and Output

Instructions are entered into a computer electronically by tapping the *keyboard*. Keyboards may be either the traditional typewriter-style (with raised keys) or flat membrane-style (with pressure-sensitive keys) not suitable for normal typing. Keyboards can be built-in or separate. More rarely, instructions can be entered by using a light pen, if one is attached, by voice commands or in other ways. This is the *input* process.

As the computer has processed whatever information has been fed in, the result, or *output*, is sent back to the user. Output can take the form of *soft copy* or *hard copy*. Soft copy is simply information displayed on the microcomputer screen or monitor, a unit which is similar to (and sometimes is) a television screen. The display on a monitor can be in color, black and white, green and, most recently, amber. A monitor generally offers better resolution than an ordinary TV screen. Hard copy refers to a paper printout that people can take away with them. It requires an additional piece of equipment, a printer. There are many types of printers that can be used with a public access system and these are discussed under "Peripherals," below.

The format of a microcomputer screen is an important consideration. Screens are measured in the number of columns or characters across and the number of lines up and down. They can display text or graphics. Most micros still come with a 40-column screen, but some machines allow for the addition of add-on circuit boards to expand to 80 columns. Eighty-column screens are preferable, particularly for word processing, since anything less makes it difficult to read the text or display it as it will ultimately be printed.

CENTRAL PROCESSING UNIT (CPU)

The *microprocessor* or *central processing unit* is the brain of the microcomputer, where arithmetic, control and logic operations occur. The CPU controls the microcomputer and therefore should be distinguished from the microcomputer itself.

A microcomputer uses a *chip* as its CPU—hence the term, "a computer on a chip." A chip is often described as a silicon wafer, which refers to its construction. This component has made the modern microcomputer possible. Chips are tiny, inexpensive circuit boards which come in various sizes. When the cabinets of most microcomputers are opened for inspection, the chips are seen lined up in rows. It is the construction and number of these chips that determine a computer's internal workspace or *memory*.

MEMORY

Memory can be divided into internal or working memory and external memory or storage (such as disk drives and tape drives, discussed under "Peripherals," below). Memory is generally measured in K, which stands for 1024 bytes. A *byte* represents one character—whether a letter, number or another symbol—of data. All data are stored digitally. A computer can only understand two states: 1 or 0, and all data are encoded as combinations of these discrete units known as binary digits, or *bits*. This is the basis of all chip technology.

In an 8-bit microprocessor, it takes eight bits to retain one byte (or one character) in memory. This is how we end up with memory that is expressed in multiples of eight: e.g., 48K, 64K, 128K, etc. The total memory is the total workspace available to the computer for the manipulation of data. In 8-bit micros, the computer processes these eight bits at one time, as a unit. Sixteen- and 32-bit machines process 16 or 32 bits, respectively, as units. This makes them much faster and capable of processing much more data than 8-bit micros.

Two principal kinds of internal memory are *ROM* (read only memory) and *RAM* (random access memory). ROM consists of programs embedded within the chip itself and cannot be changed by the user. This type of software, being part of the hardware, is called *firmware*. RAM is the main workspace available to the user. Data in RAM can be altered by the user, and therefore change frequently. Think of RAM as erasable, since it is lost (or erased) each time the computer is turned off—an important concept of which patrons should be made aware.

Some machines are referred to as having 48K, 64K, 128K, etc. of RAM memory, which gives us a basis for comparison. Since prices have been falling drastically in recent years, purchase enough RAM memory to meet the requirements of all of the software that fits into your scheme of service and is currently produced. For example, a microcomputer with disk drives should have a minimum of 64K RAM. Higher amounts of memory, such as 128K, are generally needed more for small business uses than for public access.

PERIPHERALS

Peripherals are all pieces of equipment that are not part of the computer proper, are usually external and are controlled by the computer. They include disk drives, printers and modems.

Disks and Disk Drives

Whenever the power is turned off, most microcomputers lose whatever data have been stored in the RAM (although bubble memory may ultimately change this situation). Also, the RAM can hold only one program or a limited amount of data at any one time. External *disks* are where data and programs are stored when not in use. *Disk drives* are essentially the motors that turn the disks. Since libraries can acquire as many disks as they want (or can store), disks can provide a microcomputer with virtually infinite storage capacity.

Programs can be transferred to disk and saved in *files* until needed again. Each disk is formatted electronically and broken down into concentric rings or tracks, each of which is further divided into smaller units, known as sectors.

Disks offer random access to information. An alternative is the use of *tape drives* and tapes, which must be read sequentially. For this reason, tape drives are slower and more awkward to use, and generally are not suited for public access use.

There are several types of disk drives, some more expensive than others, with advantages and disadvantages to each. It is a good idea to buy drives in pairs, because some programs require a program disk and a data disk. Two drives also make a microcomputer much more convenient to use. For the second or third public access machine in an institution, one drive may suffice.

The smallest and most inexpensive disk drive, and the kind most commonly used with microcomputers, is the 5¼-inch *floppy disk drive*. The disks themselves are called floppy disks, diskettes or floppies. Floppy disks look like small, flexible phonograph records. For use, they are inserted through a slot in the front of the disk drive and are read by a movable head.

The memory space on a floppy disk is about 100K; depending upon the computer, it can be more or less. Floppy disk drives also come in an 8-inch variety. Their additional memory capacity—a megabyte (one million bytes) or more—greatly increases the volume of data that can be online at one time.

Hard disk drives are much more expensive than floppies, but they can increase the memory space to 5, 10, 20 or more megabytes. Hard disks are usually sealed in an airtight case within the disk drive; some newer systems have removable hard disks that can be replaced. A smaller floppy drive is usually needed as a backup system for hard disk drives. Usually, a public access system will require a hard disk drive only if there are a number of micros in the same system. This forms a local network, in which many microcomputers share the same hard disk drive.

Interface Cards

To use drives and other peripherals, special circuit boards known as *interface cards* are needed. These special boards fit into the back of the microcomputer (although some systems come with certain cards built-in) and allow the micro to "communicate" with and control its peripherals.

Printers

There are two major kinds of impact printers suitable for public access: *dot matrix* and *daisy wheel*. Both are noisy. *Thermal* and other types of printers are not generally useful for public access unless a poor print quality and other problems are acceptable.

Dot Matrix and Daisy Wheel Printers

Dot matrix printers are equipped with tiny dots positioned as an array of small pins in the print head. Letters are produced as the head strikes the ribbon in a computer-directed pattern. Dot matrix printers have traditionally been inferior in print quality to daisy wheel printers, but this is changing. Generally speaking, they are less expensive than daisy wheel printers. Another advantage of a dot matrix printer is that, with various combinations of dots, it can produce graphics and different fonts (or typefaces). Some can also enlarge or reduce character size. The latter capability often allows a small dot matrix printer to produce 132 characters per line.

Daisy wheel printers get their name from the print wheel which is composed of spokes. The tip of each spoke has one print character. The wheel turns and a small hammer hits the appropriate spoke. The print quality is indistinguishable from that obtained when using a typewriter. Daisy wheel printers are sometimes called letter-quality printers. They do not produce graphics and will only print one size of type unless the print wheel is changed. Some daisy wheel printers have six or eight different typeface wheels available.

An important consideration, especially for a library, is the printer's speed, which is measured in characters per second (cps). Normally, dot matrix printers are faster. Another factor is the typeface. Some dot matrix printers use pseudo-descenders (the dots forming letters do not descend below a certain line) producing strange-looking "y"s and "p"s. A number of dot matrix printers also have a *buffer* or storage space (usually 2K) to hold data sent from the computer until they can be printed out. For some microcomputers, it is possible to purchase a larger buffer (16K or more) which will free the computer for other work while the printer continues to operate.

Paper

Paper is fed through the printer in one of two ways, either by *friction feed* or *tractor feed*. The friction-feed platen grips paper in typewriter fashion and allows the use of a single sheet of paper, such as a letterhead. Tractor-feed machines use adjustable sprockets to guide "fan-fold" or computer paper through the printer. Some machines allow for both types of paper. *Pin wheel* printers differ from tractor feed in that they have the sprockets fixed to the end of the platen and only permit one size of paper.

Number of Columns

An important characteristic of printers is the number of columns they will print. If a small business or accounting package is planned, 80 columns will not be sufficient. Accounts receivable, accounts payable and general ledger programs nearly all require 132 columns. Word processing and ordinary printing (e.g., lists, labels, etc.) require only 80 columns or less.

Noise

As mentioned earlier, all printers suitable for public access are noisy. To combat the noise element, check into an *acoustic cabinet* or *hood*. Models are available for both dot matrix and daisy wheel printers. They can easily cut noise by 80%.

Modems

Data communications or telecommunications require the use of a *modem* (modulator/demodulator), a simple translation device that allows the computer to send and receive digital code over analog telephone lines. The transmission rate is measured in *baud* and the typical baud for a home computer system is 300 (equal to 30 characters per second). Types of modems include *acoustic couplers*, which cradle the telephone in a small box, and *direct connect modems*, which use a modular phone jack to plug directly into the line. The direct connect modem eliminates the extraneous noise that the computer might mistake for incoming data. If you plan to use a modem to connect to online services such as Dialog, you will need a 1200 baud modem. Investigate to be sure one is available for the micro you plan to buy.

OPERATING SYSTEMS

Every computer must operate with a control program, or *operating system*, which regulates the flow of information and how it is stored. The *disk operating system (DOS)* runs the disk drives, keeps track of program names and where they are stored, and performs a great many other housekeeping functions. Depending upon the computer, DOS can either be stored on disk and *booted* (loaded) into RAM when the system is turned on or stored permanently in ROM.

Virtually all manufacturers have proprietary operating systems that will work only with their brand of micro. One exception to this is CP/M (Control Program for Microcomputers). CP/M is an operating system that runs on a number of different machines, provided that they have a Z-80 microprocessor. This chip can be added to a micro, usually at a cost of several hundred dollars. However, since most major microcomputers can be adapted in this way, to some extent CP/M has become a common system that is widely supported. Extensive public domain software for CP/M-based systems is excellent and inexpensive. However, one must still purchase CP/M programs in the proper format for a particular brand of microcomputer. A good source for information on CP/M software is the *CP/M Software Finder*, compiled by Digital Research ($14.95). This guide explains the origins and benefits of the CP/M operating system. It is published by Que Corp. (7999 Knue Rd., Indianapolis, IN 46250).

CP/M is a popular operating system, and a very large base of software has been written for it. However, it must be noted that the entry of IBM into the personal computer market has eroded CP/M's dominance considerably. A great deal of software is being written for MS-DOS, the operating system used by IBM machines, and it is expected that this trend will continue.

LANGUAGES

Computers receive information and instructions in one or more languages. A low-level language such as *machine language* is nearly impossible for humans to follow, but can be directly interpreted by the computer and is hence much faster for the machine to execute. An *assembler language* is an intermediate-level language, understandable by humans and used to prepare machine-language programs. A *high-level language* is in an English-like format that humans understand. Perhaps the most common is BASIC (Beginner's All-purpose Symbolic Instruction Code). BASIC is used by most people when starting out since it is a relatively simple language to learn. Specialized high-level languages include COBOL, FORTRAN, PASCAL and hundreds of others.

The software packages available today use all three levels of languages when they run on a computer. Since there are thousands of software programs for a myriad of applications, librarians do not have to do their own programming, unless they want to customize a piece of software or develop their own software for specific applications. If you do want to add one or more languages to your system after purchase, there are several things to keep in mind.

A language program won't work on just any machine. Even with BASIC, there are variations of the language, depending on the brand of micro used. To use BASIC written for one brand of micro on another brand will usually require some conversion, a task we should try to avoid. Also, some languages may require more memory capacity than others. Thus, if the library plans to add languages to the system later, it must make sure that the original equipment is expandable (i.e., that memory cards can be added).

FUNDING THE PROJECT

The next step toward starting a public access micro project is to procure funds for it. In most cases, the monies will be obtained through a grant. Most sources of funding—whether a Friends of the Library group, state agency or parent organization—will require a grant proposal, outlining purposes, budgets and so forth.

The pleasant thing about writing a proposal is that it must only be done once, although it may be revised and resubmitted if it is initially rejected. Usually, rejection has less to do with the merit of the proposal than with other factors. Often, competition for available funding can play a more important role. Do improve a grant proposal as staff knowledge increases *and* as technology changes.

The obvious place to submit a proposal is the local Friends of the Library. Such groups have been instrumental in setting up many public access projects. Other possibilities include applying to the city government for revenue sharing money, Library Services and Construction Act (LSCA) funds, and sometimes the computer companies themselves (for example, Apple, Radio Shack and others have supported some public access efforts). Chapter 5 describes two major LSCA-funded computer literacy projects: one is a statewide effort being coordinated by the California State Library; the other is a system-wide project undertaken in New York.

There are many good books around that can assist in the writing of a grant proposal (see the bibliography at the end of this book). Appendix A is a copy of an accepted grant proposal to the Friends of the Chicago Public Library. It follows the traditional proposal outline, describing needs assessment, objectives, activities, personnel/budget and evaluation.

Considering the stunning drop in the price of many computer systems over the past few years, local fundraising events, such as book sales, can sometimes bring in enough money to get started. Having a microcomputer as the goal of a book sale can stimulate a good deal of public interest.

WARNING: DON'T OVERDO IT

The development and promotion of any new library service must be done wisely, and this is particularly true of public access services. If the program is structured and marketed properly, it will serve a wide cross section of the community, making it a valuable and effective local resource. If not, the public access micro could wind up serving only a small segment of the community.

If the library offers more services than it can handle reasonably, staff rebellion and patron dissatisfaction may result. Start small, manage wisely, expand later. Listen to patrons, but don't purchase every new program or every new computer component that comes off the assembly line.

In any case, running a public access microcomputer program should never be a grim task; it should be fun and exciting. As a librarian, my personal philosophy on public access microcomputers is one of careful adventure, with the emphasis on *careful*!

The next chapter discusses how to decide what levels of service your public access project will offer and how to choose appropriate equipment.

NOTES

1. For example, the Lawrence Hall of Science on the University of California's Berkeley campus made computers available to the general public in 1972. These were not, of course, microcomputers, but teletype machines hooked up to the university's time-sharing system. Peter Hirshberg, "Compu-Tots and Other Joys of Museum Life," *Instructional Innovator* 26 (September 1981): 28.

2. It is sometimes difficult to pinpoint exactly when the first of something occurred, but the earliest public access microcomputer I know of was at White Plains (NY) Public Library in 1977. This was apparently the first experiment with coinop micro systems as well. Harold M. Shair, *Creative Computing* 3 (May/June 1977): 36.

3. James M. Kusack and John S. Bowers, "Public Microcomputers In Public Libraries," *Library Journal* 107 (November 15, 1982): 2137.

4. The first electronic bulletin board system for public use was probably the system installed at the North-Pulaski Branch Library in late 1981. Patrick R. Dewey, "Dear ABBS: Marketing, Maintenance, and Suggestions," *Small Computers In Libraries* 2 (September 1982): 1.

5. Bertha M. Cheatham, "*SLJ* News Report," in *Bowker Annual of Library Book and Trade Information, 1983*, 28th ed., ed. Joanne O'Hare (New York: R.R. Bowker, 1983).

6. Some 200 school and university libraries now have some form of this service. Robert T. Grieves, "Short Circuiting Reference Books," *Time* 121 (June 13, 1983): 76.

7. Beverly Hunter, "Computer Literacy," paper presented at the Patterns Conference on Computer Literacy, Rochester, NY (April 27-28, 1981): 3.

8. Statistics were originally reported in Patrick R. Dewey, "The Personal Computer Center At The North-Pulaski Library," *Educational Computer* 3 (March/April 1983):29.

9. Bonnie S. Fowler and Duncan Smith, "Microcomputers for the Public in the Public Library," *Information Technology and Libraries* 2 (March 1983):46.

10. *Microcomputer Hardware and Software in the El-Hi Market, 1983-87* (White Plains, NY: Knowledge Industry Publications, Inc., 1983).

2

Choosing the Micro That Meets Your Needs

While there are no hard and fast formulas librarians can use for choosing a microcomputer for public access, there are at least a few guidelines they can follow to help them select from among the bewildering array of hardware and software on the market. This chapter will concentrate on hardware. Chapter 3 will discuss software selection.

BASIC PRINCIPLES OF SELECTION

First, it is important to distinguish between a micro selected for internal library chores and one intended for use by patrons, many of them beginners. A micro for library use is usually dedicated to a specific task, such as circulation backup or generation of catalog cards, overdue notices, etc. A public access micro must function in a much more flexible way. In fact, it can be thought of as a hobbyist model because, like hobbyists, patrons will either know what the micro does or will be struggling to figure it out. Except in the rarest or simplest of cases (e.g., if the level of service is limited to providing a programmed game), experimentation will be broad and diverse. The micro will be used by all elements of the community.

Hardware should never be selected in a vacuum. The decision should be made based upon a combination of factors, including: available funding, the level of expertise and enthusiasm of patrons and staff, the time available for the project and the scope of the public access effort. Of these, the project's scope—i.e., the level(s) of service that the library will provide—will play a major role, since it will determine the software and hardware capabilities needed. Planning and good judgment, including a needs assessment, should not be neglected at the early stages. Don't risk becoming one of the many who don't need, don't want or can't use the computer that they bought.

Libraries must also consider the availability of local computer clubs, volunteers, vendor support, peripherals and accessories when they figure out which package of "nuts and bolts" to buy. Finally, they must consider change.

Computer software and hardware change and are upgraded all the time; even now, compatibility interfaces for major microcomputers are beginning to sprout up and may, once again, quickly change the whole ballgame. As people use and become familiar with a microcomputer, their needs also change and become more sophisticated. This shifting landscape has led to one central theme in public access micro hardware selection: *expandability*. Don't be lulled into thinking that a particular consumer electronic item will be the rage forever. Like library books and facilities, they must be replaced and rebuilt. It is important to select a micro system that can have new features added to it as needs arise.

As librarians, the difficulty of selecting the right system is compounded when we are called on a Friday afternoon and told that we must have a plan or proposal for spending "X" number of dollars on microcomputer equipment by Monday. It's a common problem. In the worst possible case, a microcomputer will just show up in the office or library like an abandoned child, sometimes for use by an unwilling staff.

The balance of this chapter presents a framework for determining public access needs and choosing appropriate hardware. It can also be used as an aid in writing a proposal. It covers the following "basics":

1. Determining the scope of the public access project;
2. Selecting equipment for different levels of service;
3. Purchasing a micro system.

Each will be discussed in turn.

SCOPE OF THE PUBLIC ACCESS EFFORT

As noted earlier, an important step in initiating a public access program is to determine the scope of the project, i.e., to determine what level(s) of service the library wants to provide. *Know what you want your computer to do before you buy it*. This is the most often-repeated caveat applied to micro purchases, and it pertains to libraries and consumers alike. In addition, the library must consider its own resources in terms of available staff and facilities.

Determining Patron Interest and Needs

Surveys, seminars, even circulation figures, can be used to find out what patrons are interested in and how much they know about computers. When preparing a survey to measure the computer literacy level in the community, emphasize microcomputer applications. Focus on the various services that can be provided with such a machine: e.g., writing and editing term papers and reports (word processing), figuring out the family budget (spreadsheets), sorting and updating mailing lists (data base management), self-study programs (computer-assisted instruction), etc. By concentrating on micro applications (in terms patrons can understand), the library will get a truer feel for community needs and interests.

Previous experience with computers, ability to type and how often patrons would use the public access micro are other areas that the survey should address. Make some of the survey questions essays, allowing for the input of more than yes-or-no type answers. Also, attempt to determine what percentage of regular library users already own micros.

Another way to gather information is to hold a seminar on a computer application—for example, word processing—and then measure the response. Poll the people who attend to see why they came and how many of them own some micro equipment.

It is also possible to gauge public interest by checking circulation figures for computer books. Also, check whether interlibrary loan requests include large numbers of computer titles and, if so, on what topics.

The library service population should also be analyzed. It is important to know, for example, whether the community is composed primarily of elderly people, has a large proportion of children, etc. This information, together with the data gathered by the various polling techniques, forms the basis for any decisions that will be made regarding the type of public access service to be offered.

Staff Availability

A major factor in the selection process (and one often overlooked) involves a realistic appraisal of just how much staff time is available for the project. It is important not to detract from other important library responsibilities.

Each new microcomputer-related service will require some staff involvement. The amount of staff time that such a project could involve is open-ended. Some of the principal jobs that a public access project will create are: distributing diskettes; selecting and maintaining software; checking software and/or machines in and out, if they circulate; offering routine orientation and assistance to most patrons (this can vary greatly); and making appointments. (Chapter 4 discusses the issue of staff time and management in detail.)

How Much Space Is Available?

To some extent, the scope of the public access project will be determined by the facilities available. For example, if you only have space for one computer, where would you put a second one? Factors such as this may be self-limiting. Obviously, if the library has only a small room or reading area available, it cannot house 20 machines. Or, if the micro must be located in the main reading room, a noisy printer might be out of the question.

COMPARING LEVELS OF SERVICE, EQUIPMENT AND COSTS

Once you have a clear idea of the types of public access services the library will provide, it helps to know what different levels of hardware can do. It is also necessary to have a realistic idea of what "X" number of dollars will purchase. Today's microcomputers offer several definable hardware levels. However, the number of potential add-on features is formidable, and the lines of demarcation can quickly become blurred. Some machines will support more software levels (and therefore, levels of service) than others, so it is important to keep the options open. Do not buy a machine that is a dead end, i.e., one that isn't expandable. Following are some rough classifications of equipment and their capabilities. These are summarized in Table 2.1.

Table 2.1: Comparison of Micro Equipment and Capabilities

Price Range*	Peripherals and Memory	Purpose (level of service)	Example
$20-$50	ROM only	Simple spelling/math	Speak N' Spell
$30-$500	1 Tape drive, 1-32K RAM	Simple computer literacy, lending hardware	Timex-Sinclair, Commodore VIC 20
$2000-$3000	1 Disk drive, 48-64K RAM	Advanced literacy, spreadsheets, word processing	Apple IIe, Atari 800, IBM PCjr, Macintosh, TRS-80
$3000-$5000	2 Disk drives, modem (300 baud), printer, 64K RAM	Bulletin board system, online services, wall charts, lending software, supports higher-level languages such as COBOL, FORTRAN, etc.	Apple IIe, Commodore SuperPET, IBM PC
More than $5000	Hard disk drive, 132 column printer, modem (300+ baud), 2 disk drives, 128K RAM (and up)	Business use (accounting, etc.)	Apple III, IBM PC, Commodore CBM 8032

*Prices are as of late 1983.

Preprogrammed Microchip Products

Speak N' Spell and similar microchip devices are perhaps the simplest form of equipment that has been tried in a public library. Because electronics prices have been declining rapidly in recent years, these products can be obtained for less than $50. They are generally used for simple computer-assisted instruction, such as providing spelling practice for elementary school children. Speak N' Spell and similar devices are not programmable by the user; they are preprogrammed for a specific purpose by the manufacturer.

Simple Computer Systems

The simplest computer systems, such as the Timex-Sinclair, the Commodore 64 or PET, and the VIC 20, can be purchased from as little as $30 up to $600, without drives or monitor. These machines are most suitable for lending to patrons and are most useful for simple computer literacy projects (e.g., elementary programming practice) and computer awareness. Some of these systems have options that can be added later, for increased capabilities. The Commodore 64, for example, is an expandable machine, since drives and other accessories can be added later if desired. The PET has the monitor and tape drive built into the machine.

Medium Range Systems

A medium range system is usually a one drive, 64K RAM machine, such as an Apple IIe, Macintosh, IBM PCjr and others. Prices range from $2000 to $3000. This level allows for the use of nearly all available software. However, word processing and data base management will be inefficient on such systems unless a printer is added. Generally, one can be added for $500 or more.

Complete Systems

For a complete system, two disk drives, a minimum of 64K RAM and a printer are required. A modem is optional unless some sort of online service is planned. For such a configuration, $3000 to $5000 (or more) per unit will be typical, depending upon the accessories purchased. Also in this category are small business machines such as the Apple III and IBM PC.

Of course, prices and technical data change very quickly, so it will be necessary to investigate current prices. Computer magazines are a good place to start, as are local computer stores. Word of mouth is always valuable, so talk to others who have already purchased a microcomputer. Also, libraries can often get the school price for equipment from dealers, so they should ask around—the discount can be considerable.

IMPORTANT SELECTION CRITERIA

The flood of micro systems and accessories on the market makes it very difficult to know just how much is enough for your library's applications, and how much is too much. The following questions should be considered when establishing criteria for selection.

Is the machine expandable? Machines that cannot be expanded, or can be expanded but only at great expense, should be avoided unless a limited application is planned. For example, machines purchased for lending to patrons will probably not need upgrading.

Is there a wide and easily accessible range of software? Regardless of how much a micro is capable of doing in terms of its hardware, it can do nothing without proper software. Any machine deficient in this area will be unattractive for all but the simplest levels of service.

Will word processing be featured? If so, an 80-column display screen is almost a necessity. Upper and lower case, as well as a printer, should also be installed at the time of purchase. The micro must also have at least one disk drive.

Will the micro support CP/M-based programs? It is often worthwhile to purchase a machine that can handle CP/M or that can be adapted by means of an add-on circuit board (see Chapter 1) to support CP/M. CP/M-based programs allow for many applications that are not possible with the basic software.

Is there a large choice of peripherals available? One rule of thumb is to take note of the flow of peripherals on the market for a particular micro. A number of good systems have handy slots built into the chassis for expansion or interface cards.

Does the micro have a modem? If any sort of online services are planned, a modem will be needed. Make sure one can be added to the micro you purchase.

Is the documentation good? Do not check only the manuals that come with the machine; there should be a selection of manuals, available separately, that have been produced by the manufacturer or other companies.

Does the machine have a standard keyboard? Do not settle for a substandard keyboard either in the size of the keys or their arrangement. It should not be any more difficult to type at the computer than at a regular typewriter. No one needs membrane keyboards for public access.

Will software be circulated? If you decide primarily to circulate software, then the micro that will be used for copying programs must have at least two drives. Also, if a large quantity of good public domain software can be obtained cheaply for a particular micro, then you may want to buy a machine to match the treasure trove.

Do clubs or user groups exist? Find out whether any local computer clubs have been created for the computer under consideration. These groups are a good source of information to go to with questions, problems or to learn about how others are using the machines. They are also a primary source of public domain programs.

Will the name be recognized? Since we wish to attract users, it often helps to have a brand name that patrons recognize. A machine with a well-known name can help to eliminate much of the fear and confusion of first-time patrons. Of course, this can occasionally backfire—for example, if the company goes out of business.

Where will the machine be serviced? Check on how or where the micro will be repaired. A vendor may or may not provide adequate repair and maintenance service. Some machines must *still* be sent away! Examine service contracts thoroughly, and do not settle for less than a 90-day warranty on a new machine.

SOME GENERAL BUYING ADVICE

It is much easier to let the dealer install features such as upper and lower case capability at the time of purchase than it is to return the machine later. In general, it's best to acquire all the basic components you need at one time.

There is not much need for *joysticks* or *paddles,* those little external control gadgets that make arcade games so much fun. Even if they could be justified for use, they cannot be kept in repair. Many libraries have made efforts to install paddles without much success. At North-Pulaski, the paddle set was repaired four times before it was abandoned.

A color monitor is not a necessity, but it will add a lot to the project. It does not usually require a great deal of added expense. However, make certain that the clarity of the text on a color screen is up to the required standards.

Above all else, *avoid* impulse buying, "bargains" or hardware/software combinations that might prove costly, especially if the software is not needed. Do not purchase a machine that stands a chance of becoming obsolete rapidly. If the firm has declared bankruptcy, do not purchase the computer no matter how attractive the price is: Who will repair it? How will you get software, etc.? Vendor support and service are important considerations and must not be treated lightly.

The following section presents brief profiles of several major microcomputer manufacturers and their equipment.

THUMBNAIL SKETCHES OF MAJOR MICROCOMPUTERS

The following major microcomputers have generally performed well for public access. Some machines are no longer being manufactured and have been replaced. It is probable that the newer models will also work well for public access, but as yet they remain untested for use in libraries. We will attempt only a brief description, including a list of software sources, for each machine. One good source of more detailed information is the *Data Pro Directory of Small Computers,* which outlines several hundred small computer systems. The bibliography at the end of this book lists other resources. Evaluations and reviews are to be found in many current magazines and special reports. Addresses for the manufacturers discussed below are given in Appendix B. Additional software sources are listed in Chapter 3 and in Appendix C.

The prices and specifications given below are as of late 1983. Changes are to be expected, and readers should contact the individual manufacturers at the time of purchase.

Apple Computer

More libraries have chosen the Apple II computer than any other brand. (The Apple I was sold as a kit that had to be assembled.) The Apple II has a reputation as a reliable machine. There is more software available for it than for any other microcomputer around, although the entry of IBM into the market may change this picture. Eventually, the Apple II+ took the place of the Apple II, but this has now been replaced by the Apple IIe. The new model promises more for the beginner, including (for a small extra fee) an 80-column display format and 128K RAM memory. It also comes with lower case, extra function keys and conforms to the IBM Selectric keyboard format.

The Apple IIe is known as the hobbyist model—moderately priced but with full features. The Apple IIe Language System allows for the introduction of PASCAL, FORTRAN and COBOL. The Apple IIe supports most of the software available for the model II.

The Apple III is meant as a small business machine, but it will support most of the software available for the IIe simply at the flip of a switch. It has a built-in 140K floppy disk drive, a 13-key numeric keypad, programmable function keys and 128K bytes of RAM memory, expandable to 256K. Another feature (not available for the Apple IIe) is a built-in earphone jack which will mute the normal speaker output of the computer. The languages supported include Apple III PASCAL and Apple III COBOL. An annual maintenance agreement is available through many licensed dealers.

In January 1984 Apple introduced the Macintosh, a new 32-bit computer. The basic Macintosh, with 128K of memory, a high-resolution black-and-white screen and one disk drive (3½-inch, compared with the traditional 5¼-inch), is expected to cost $2500, and will weigh slightly less than 20 pounds. The micro will have a proprietary operating system and will come with two programs initially: MacPaint, which will allow users to draw images on the screen, and MacWrite, a word processing program.

Software information sources for the Apple: *The Addison-Wesley Book of Apple Computer Software* ($19.95) has very understandable, thorough and lengthy reviews. A critical rating system (A, B, C, etc.) helps the reader in the selection process. Available from: The Book Co., 11223 S. Hindry Ave., Los Angeles, CA 90045.

The *Bluebook for the Apple Computer* ($24.95) contains more than 4600 actual programs along with manufacturers' descriptions. It also lists peripheral hardware available for Apple and Apple-compatible computers. A good place to start. Available from: WIDL Video Publications, 5245 W. Diversey Ave., Chicago, IL 60639.

Swift's Educational Software Directory ($18.95) is published for the Apple II. Entries are listed by title and subject and are broken down under the headings elementary school, middle school, high school, community college, university and continuing education. Available from: Sterling Swift Publishing Co., 7901 South IH-35, Austin, TX 78744.

Atari Home Computer

Atari, Inc., a division of Warner Communications Co., began distributing its home computers in 1979, with the introduction of the Atari 400 and Atari 800 microcomputers.

The Atari 400 has 16K bytes of RAM; the Atari 800 has 16K, expandable to 48K. The 800 can also handle up to four 88K disk drives. The 400 has a membrane-style (flat) keyboard, not suitable for normal typing, whereas the 800 has a regular typewriter-style keyboard. The 400 must be used with a TV rather than a monitor, but the 800 can be used with either.

Both versions come with a built-in RF modulator, upper and lower case, and three dot matrix printer options. Both systems use convenient ROM cartridge slots; the 800 has two of them. Either system can accommodate an acoustic modem and game controls. Numerous software packages have emerged over the past few years. Languages supported include PILOT (with turtle graphics), Atari BASIC and ASSEMBLER. One thousand factory-authorized service centers have been established.

Atari is no longer manufacturing the 400 and 800 micros; however it will continue to support the systems. To replace them, Atari has introduced the 600XL and 800XL micros. The 600XL has 16K RAM (expandable to 64K); the 800XL has 64K. Both have a typewriter-style keyboard, built-in Atari BASIC programming language and a screen format of 40 columns by 24 lines. The 600XL is used with a TV rather than a monitor; the 800XL can use either.

Software information sources for the Atari: *The Addison-Wesley Book of Atari Computer Software* ($19.95) is similar to the *Addison-Wesley Book of Apple Computer Software,* described above. Available from: The Book Co., 11223 S. Hindry Ave., Los Angeles, CA 90045.

The *Bluebook for the Atari Computer* ($17.95) is similar to the *Bluebook for the Apple Computer,* above. Available from: WIDL Video Publications, 5245 W. Diversey Ave., Chicago, IL 60639.

Commodore Business Machines

The five machines discussed below show the wide range of options available to today's microcomputer shopper. All machines have disk drives, printers and modems available as options.

The Commodore VIC 20 has been advertised recently for less than $100. The screen is 22 columns by 23 lines. An RF modulator and TV switchbox are included, with 16-color output available. The micro has 5K of RAM, expandable to 32K. The VIC 20 has been lent successfully to patrons. (See the Portsmouth Public Library discussion in Chapter 5.)

The Commodore 64 is equipped with 64K RAM and has an optional add-on Z-80 plug-in cartridge which allows the use of many CP/M-based programs. It also comes with upper and lower case and extra function keys. The screen is 40 columns by 25 lines and 16 colors are available.

The Commodore PET 4032 has 32K of RAM and includes the CRT. Unlike the original PET, it has a standard typewriter-style keyboard and numeric keypad. It has upper and lower case and a screen format of 40 columns by 25 lines.

The Commodore SuperPET has 96K of RAM and will allow the addition of 5 to 7.5 Megabyte hard disk systems. It comes with upper and lower case and has a screen format of 80 columns by 25 lines. Languages supported are ASSEMBLER, WATERLOO, microAPL, microFORTRAN, microPASCAL, microBASIC and microCOBOL.

The Commodore CBM 8032 had 64K of RAM. Its screen format is 80 columns by 25 lines including upper and lower case. It supports ASSEMBLER, BASIC and PASCAL Development Package.

A maintenance agreement is available for all machines through TRW Inc., 23555 Euclid Ave., Cleveland, OH 44117.

Software information sources for Commodore micros: The *Bluebook for the Commodore Computer* ($17.95) is similar to the *Apple Bluebook*, described above. Available from: WIDL Video Publications, 5245 W. Diversey Ave., Chicago, IL 60639.

Commodore Software Encyclopedia ($9.95) is a modestly priced directory of approximately 1000 programs. Available from: Commodore Business Machines, Inc., 1200 Wilson Dr., West Chester, PA 19380.

IBM PC

This big-name computer company has a lively marketing strategy and an established customer base, which may account for the instant popularity of the IBM Personal Computer. Two models of the IBM PC are available from dealers: the IBM PC and the IBM PC XT. The machines differ mainly in disk storage. The PC comes with 64K of RAM, expandable to 640K, and 5 expansion slots. It can accommodate a maximum of two disk drives available in 180K or 360K. The PC XT has 128K of RAM, expandable to 640K, and 8 expansion slots. It comes with a 360K disk drive and a 10 Megabyte fixed disk, which is not available for the PC. Both machines have 40K of ROM.

Options available for both models include a detachable keyboard and a built-in BASIC interpreter. Languages supported include ASSEMBLER, COBOL, FORTRAN and PASCAL. A CP/M card is available. Service and warranty options include IBM Personal Computer Service Agreement, Warranty Extension Option and Annual Option.

In late 1983 IBM introduced the PCjr (first called the "Peanut") which is expected to be available in mid-1984. This is a lower-cost machine, available in two versions. The entry level model (which will sell for about $700) comes with 64K of RAM and accepts cartridge programs only. It has a 40-line screen display and can handle 16 colors. The higher-priced model (set at $1269) has 128K of RAM and can accept both cartridges and diskettes for running programs. The display format is 80 lines with 16-color output.

Both machines come with a flat, lightweight keyboard which generated considerable discussion at the machine's introduction—much of it critical. The oblong keys operate on a spring return and do not facilitate touch-typing. However, all of the keyboard's 62 keys are programmable and are designed so that various templates can be placed over the keyboard.

Options for both machines include a monitor (a TV set can also be used) an internal modem, and a thermal printer or the IBM PC Color printer (which requires a printer attachment). A maximum of one disk drive can be added to either machine.

Software information sources for IBM micros: *The Addison-Wesley Book of IBM Computer Software* ($19.95) is similar to the *Addison-Wesley Apple Book* described above. Available from: The Book Co., 11223 S. Hindry Ave., Los Angeles, CA 90045.

The *Bluebook for the IBM Computer* ($24.95) is similar to the *Apple Bluebook*, above, except for the price. Available from: WIDL Video Publications, 5245 W. Diversey Ave., Chicago, IL 60639.

Texas Instruments

The TI99/4A is the basic popular model that has been used in libraries. The 16-bit microprocessor affords the user 16K bytes of RAM and 16K of ROM. The system can support disk drives, thermal printer and modem, and has an add-on 32K expansion module. The unit originally sold for less than $100. Many hundreds of programs are available. Servicing for minor problems, and some hardware exchange, can be obtained at local consumer group exchange centers; major repair work must be sent to the factory. By the end of 1983 Texas Instruments will be out of the home computer market. While Texas Instruments has promised to continue to support the machine, this would now be a poor choice for a library, since too many factors—especially software production—are uncertain.

Timex-Sinclair

The Timex-Sinclair 1000 is the cheapest computer available as of late 1983. Its list price is $49.95, and many dealers now sell it for less than $30. If the library decides to make computers available for patrons to take home, this is a likely candidate. The Downers Grove Public Library (see Chapter 5) has done this with excellent results. There are also very large and active user groups that share information on the Timex-Sinclair.

The Timex-Sinclair 1000 has 2K of RAM, expandable to 16K, and a built-in VHF-RF demodulator. The language supported is BASIC. In late 1983 Timex announced that a telecommunications option was available. A low-cost annual service contract is available.

Software information sources for the Timex-Sinclair: The *Timex-Sinclair 1983 Directory* ($5.00) includes information about the peripherals and software available for this computer. The book contains photographs and lists suppliers. Available from: E. Arthur Brown Co., 1702 Oak Knoll Dr., Alexandria, MN 56308.

TRS-80

The TRS-80 is produced by Tandy Corp. and sold through Radio Shack. As with the Apple, the TRS-80 has built a large and loyal following over the past five years, making a sizable pool of software available. The models listed below come with a video monitor and a wide range of options including modems and printers.

Tandy began production of microcomputers in 1977 with the TRS-80 Model I. The machine offered 4K of RAM, expandable to 48K. The Model I was replaced by the Model II, a micro primarily aimed at the business community. The TRS-80 II comes with 64K of RAM, and has a screen display of 80 columns by 24 lines, including upper and lower case. It comes with an 8-inch floppy disk drive, but will accommodate a hard disk system. ASSEMBLER, BASIC, COBOL and GRAPHICS languages are supported.

The TRS-80 III has 48K of RAM and a screen display of either 32 or 64 characters by 24 lines (depending on the version chosen) and upper and lower case. It comes with two disk drives. ASSEMBLER, BASIC, COBOL, FORTRAN and PASCAL are supported.

As of late 1983 the TRS-80 II and III were no longer being manufactured, and were replaced by the TRS-80 Model 4. The Model 4 has 64K of RAM, expandable to 128K. The display is 80 characters by 24 lines, upper and lower case. The micro can be purchased with one or two disk drives, and it supports the same languages as the TRS-80 III. A package is available which upgrades the TRS-80 III to the TRS-80 4. Service is available from any Radio Shack Computer Center for all machines.

Software information sources for TRS micros: The *Applications Software Sourcebook* ($4.95) contains over 3900 program listings. It may be obtained at most Radio Shack Computer Centers or through the Radio Shack Education Division, 400 Atrium, One Tandy Center, Fort Worth, TX 76102.

COINOP COMPANIES

A few vendors supply coin-operated equipment to libraries that wish to charge for services (Chapter 4 discusses charging for public access services in more detail). Typically, the equipment is supplied free by the vendor who then collects the proceeds—much like any vending machine operation. In some cases, a revenue-sharing arrangement can be worked out, or the library can lease the equipment and keep the proceeds, etc. At present the following companies offer computer vending services for libraries. Addresses are given in Appendix D.

Perhaps the best known system is CompuVend, from Gaylord Brothers, Inc. The equipment (which the library leases) consists of an Apple II with dual disk drives, a printer and a color monitor. The vending equipment comes with a two-key security system, and each library can set its own rate of charge.

TAVA Corp. offers two options: outright purchase of equipment, and a plan in which

The CompuVend coinop micro workstation. Coins are inserted in the box, right. Courtesy Gaylord Brothers, Inc.

the library pays nothing and receives 20% of the gross revenue from machines that TAVA installs. TAVA provides an Apple IIe micro with two drives, a dot matrix printer and its own security system.

Maxwell Library Systems at Boston Copico provides public access micros, along with hardware and software for library functions. The package, which is free to the library, includes either an Apple IIe or TRS-80 Model 4 microcomputer, disk drives, a printer and a supply of business and educational software. Users are charged $2.50 per hour for encoded cards which allow up to ten hours of computer time. Maxwell collects the proceeds once a month.

Computer Mart of New Hampshire sells a coinbox for $400 which has been installed at more than 20 locations. Patrons buy 15-minute tokens from the library. The equipment can accept several tokens at the beginning of a session—for example, a patron can insert four tokens at the outset and work uninterrupted for an hour. A problem with this arrangement is that in some cases you must turn the computer off in order to go on to another program. When the machine is turned off a new token must be inserted and all remaining time is forfeited. The package comes with 100 tokens, cables and an interface card. The firm also has lease and other arrangements for computer equipment.

Micro Timesharing used to offer a lease arrangement, but now makes coinop Apple computers available for sale only.

WARRANTY AND SERVICE CONTRACT

Microcomputers are generally rugged but, as with all machinery, the equipment will eventually break down. For most libraries, a local vendor (usually the place where the equipment was purchased) will furnish an annual service contract or will provide maintenance. If the machines are bolted down, or if it is difficult to get them to a shop, consider an on-site service contract, available for certain machines.

Most machines come with a three month warranty. Therefore, the service contract should begin on the day the warranty expires. Make sure that all important components are serviceable by one vendor.

HOW TO DEAL WITH A DEALER

The most important thing to remember regarding dealers is: Do not go to a dealer expecting him to help you choose the micro best for you. The job of a dealer is selling, not helping, since volume of sales determines profit. Dealers are busy and do not have time to answer more than the simplest questions. In most cases, assistance will be minimal and pressure to purchase can be enormous.

The key is to be well-informed *before* going to a dealer. Analyze your needs, read any available literature, talk to other micro users and other libraries with micro programs. Then you will be able to visit a computer store and tell the dealer what you want, instead of taking whatever happens to be on sale that week.

There are two types of dealers: full service and no service. It is important to have a good relationship with a dealer who provides software and adequate maintenance. A good dealer will service your equipment even if he didn't sell it to you.

Computer stores can be a place to get information, but they are usually not the best place. Some stores are little more than a hole in the wall, with a shelf for books and a few tables for equipment. Others are better stocked with extensive software and a knowledgeable staff. Remember: From our point of view, a computer store is as good as its service, not its sales!

SUMMARY

There are many microcomputers and peripherals available which offer a wide range of capabilities for public access. As we have emphasized, the applications for which the micro is intended should dictate which machine is ultimately selected. This chapter has presented some guidelines for selecting levels of service and appropriate micro systems. In Chapter 3, we turn to the crucial issue of software—the heart of any public access micro program.

3

Choosing and Evaluating Software

It has been said that "a computer can do anything!" An overstatement, of course, but a computer can do many things very well, *if* the right software can be found. The opposite is also painfully true: "A computer can do nothing without software."

The right mix of software can make a library's public access microcomputer program flourish. A poor selection can result in anything from turning the library into an arcade to killing public interest in the project entirely.

This chapter sets forth the areas of software selection that should be considered for a public access program. It lists a number of programs that libraries have found to be successful. The emphasis throughout is on what constitutes good software for public access and where to find it.

WHAT IS SOFTWARE?

As explained in Chapter 1, software or computer programs are simply sets of instructions that tell the computer what to do. For example, here is a simple BASIC program:

```
10 PRINT "HELLO"
20 GOTO 10
```

This program is extremely short, but it will cause the word "HELLO" to be printed infinitely by looping the computer back to the "PRINT" statement in line 10. The computer executes each instruction in order, beginning with the lowest line number, in this case 10.

Some programs consist of thousands of such statements and are incredibly complex, taking months or even years to write. In this chapter we will be taking the "black box" approach to computers and software—i.e., it does not matter to us *how* it works, as long as it works! This is a perfectly valid approach, since people use things all the time—televisions, microwave ovens, etc.—without understanding the actual mechanics involved.

In the same way, it is not necessary for most librarians to take up programming. We are fast entering the age of the computer users rather than the programmers. In the early days of computing, one had to know programming in order to communicate with mainframes and minicomputers. However, with the dawn of the microcomputer, more and more packaged programs have become available for a host of applications. Today, professional programmers and software houses have done much of the work, although customizing a program from time to time to fit individual requirements may be challenging and fun.

This chapter deals with the applications software that patrons will use in the library. It is not concerned with systems software, which was discussed in Chapter 1.

SOMETHING FOR EVERYONE: AN OVERRIDING PRINCIPLE

As librarians, the manner in which we select software for a public access project should reflect one of the same characteristics often required in the selection of books in a public library—variety.

Variety means more than different kinds, it means levels as well. Age, educational level, reading level and interests, such as hobbies, all play a role. Table 3.1 lists the programs chosen by 100 consecutive computer users at the North-Pulaski Branch Library. It illustrates the wide diversity of use by patrons.

Table 3.1: North-Pulaski Computer Use, May 1983

Program	Number of Users
Brought their own	11
Chess	3
Computer programming	19
Data base management	5
Education	6
Games	12
Keyboard for beginners	15
Miscellaneous or assorted	7
Typing	3
Utility	3
Word processing	9
Spreadsheet/advanced	3
None (used manual or book)	4
Total	100

Source: North-Pulaski Branch Library.

The statistics presented in Table 3.1 emphasize the importance of having a balanced software collection for public access. Of course, it is no more necessary for a library to have every piece of software written for every application than it is for the same library to have every book published in its collection. Rather, a library should strive to include good programs in each of the areas of service it wishes to provide. In some cases, for example data base management, one good program may suffice; in others, for example entertainment, many programs will be needed. The following section discusses the areas of software selection to consider for public access. Some examples of specific programs are included. More specific programs are described later in this chapter in the section "Good Programs for Public Libraries."

AREAS OF SOFTWARE SELECTION

We can easily identify the following specific areas of software selection for a public library. Keep in mind that we are selecting public access software and not software for internal library use.

Computer Literacy or Awareness

This is generally the greatest area of usefulness in a public library. In a sense, all software contributes to a person's understanding of how a computer works and what it can do. There are, however, specific pieces of explanatory software that are designed to help patrons learn how to use a micro.

A keyboard program is a handy time-saver for introducing first-time users to the microcomputer. It tutors users in the basic functions of a computer keyboard. It is an interactive program—i.e., the user proceeds through the program at his own pace and receives different types of instruction based on his responses. A good keyboard program will use high resolution graphics to draw an outline of a keyboard on the screen.

There are other good introductory programs that teach the fundamentals of running and operating software, and these should be included in software purchases in this area. Keyboard and other introductory programs exist for all major micros.

Programming

As long as your micro is equipped with one or more languages, patrons can do their own programming. In addition, there are programs specifically designed for beginners. People like to try programming in BASIC, PASCAL or other computer languages. Programs such as Step by Step and Teacher Plus, both elementary BASIC programming tutorials, provide an entry point for beginners. Many beginners think that they will produce all of their own software, but quickly discover the world of ready-made programs.

Computer-assisted Instruction (CAI)

CAI programs are generally used in conjunction with classes run at the same time, either by the library or by local schools. General Education Development (GED) and English as a Second Language (ESL) are two examples. Students can supplement their work at the public access micro. Programs should be chosen in consultation with whoever is in charge of the curriculum. Reading skills, spelling programs, elementary math and others fall into this category. Many individuals will also wish to pursue various categories of computer-assisted instruction independently.

Special-interest Programs

These are programs that cover a variety of everyday, practical applications. They include software for tax preparation, accounting, recipe-doubling, plant care and more. Many patrons are likely to develop their own programs.

Library Skills

This is really part of the CAI category, but it is listed separately because of its obvious interest and importance to libraries. Included here are programs explaining the use of the card catalog, the Dewey Decimal System or other library-related items. These are good to have on hand for students referred from schools or for anyone else who wants a greater understanding of the library.

Unfortunately, there are not many library skills programs around. Calico offers library skills programs for the Apple. Units include instruction on the library catalog, periodicals index, poetry indexes and almanacs, and more are promised. The programs are generally good, with a self-paced, tutorial approach, and the user receives ample explanation of wrong answers.

Classic Library Programs, available from Right On Programs, includes 12 different CAI library skills programs. Programs include Learning about Catalog Cards, Learning to Understand the Card Catalog, Advanced Dewey Decimal System, Dictionary Skills, Learning to Understand Copyright Notice and Basic Fiction Skills.

A program called Library Skills, from Micro Power and Light Co., is a good example of a poor use of a computer. Instead of any true interaction between learner and computer, the material is mostly displayed on the screen page by page. In short, the material could be learned just as well using a book. Students are likely to be bored.

Data Base Management

A data base management system (DBMS) allows the user to store, manipulate and retrieve a group of facts and figures. The concepts here are not exactly new to most librarians. However, the microcomputer has made these functions available to libraries and the general public at the tapping of a few keys instead of the hours or days such projects might take if done manually. Data base management systems excel in sorting and resorting, alphabetically and numerically, lists of figures and facts. Such systems are getting better all the time.

Patrons may use DBMS programs to create mailing lists and the like; the library can also use them to provide a number of innovative services for patrons. For example, at North-Pulaski, a Subject Guide Wall Chart was produced with a data base management system (see Chapter 7). The chart lists the most frequently asked-for subject headings along with their corresponding Dewey Decimal and Library of Congress Classification numbers. Without the micro and DBMS software, such a project would have been impossible because of the manpower needed.

A few of the specifics to look for when choosing a DBMS include sort time (some can be very slow) and the number of fields and records possible. The entire data base is termed a *file* (some systems, in fact, are called file cabinets). Some of the original systems would not store more than the amount of data which could be loaded into RAM, severely limiting the amount of storage in any single file.

Data base management systems are either designed for a particular job (e.g., for producing mailing labels) or customized to perform several functions. Customized versions are usually much more expensive, but will perform many more tasks. Programs for specific jobs are usually simpler and require less time to set up.

Every library with a data base management system can count on attracting patrons who want to set up a mailing list. This is fine as long as the library establishes some rules. Patrons must bring their own data diskettes and be made aware that the library is not responsible for lost data. Further, patrons cannot be guaranteed any regular time on the computer for their projects. On the other hand, once a patron has completed the initial setup and input, he or she may only have to make a monthly visit to update the file or to produce a printout.

Patrons should be responsible for their own labels, paper and other supplies, unless the library wishes to assume the burden. Selling such materials in small packages may provide needed support income and will be convenient for patrons at the same time.

Ideally, the library should offer several simple data base systems, including those that children might be able to use. A number of good, simple programs are to be found in public domain software libraries.

One flexible, menu-diven data base system that is commercially available is The Data Factory. An advantage of this system is that, for a small amount, a yearly warranty contract can be purchased. The contract provides for unlimited replacement copies (if the originals go bad) and software updates. The system is usually, though not always, updated each year.

FCM—Filing, Cataloging and Mailing (formerly First Class Mail)—is a good program for producing customized mailing lists and labels. It does not require as much set-up time as some other data base management systems.

There are data base management systems available for every major microcomputer, and they are frequently reviewed in the literature.

Word Processing

On the whole, libraries provide word processing software at a public access site for demonstration purposes. Some libraries have made word processing equipment available for actual patron use, for example, by students working on term papers. A word processor is the modern electronic equivalent of the typewriter. Text can by typed into RAM, saved on disk, retrieved and displayed at a later time and printed out in original or revised format.

Children, too, seem aware that word processors may eventually replace typewriters. Such programs as Atariwriter are suitable for children, and inexpensive. If possible, get simple, medium and advanced programs.

It is not mandatory to have an 80-column display format to run a word processing program, but it's advisable if the finished product is to be seen before it is printed out. Some newer programs such as Screenwriter or Superscribe will produce 70 columns on a 40-column screen without any additional hardware, so investigate.

Many microcomputer word processing programs now come with "spellers" (features that correct spelling), math modules and other sophisticated add-ons. A speller program is good for demonstration purposes.

Many believe WordStar to be the best word processing package available for microcomputers, but it requires a micro that uses the CP/M operating system, which is an added expense. Perhaps the best non-CP/M word processing software for the Apple and IBM is Pie Writer (the newer version is called Pie 2.2). The program comes with a hands-on screen tutorial and excellent detailed documentation. Whichever word processing program you choose, make sure you have several books, especially tutorials, available for patrons to consult.

Electronic Spreadsheets

The spreadsheet is the modern version of the accountant's or mathematician's worksheet. It is sometimes described as the "what if" program, since it allows the user to enter a number of variables. The program automatically recalculates the resultant changes.

VisiCalc is the best known of all the spreadsheet software. It is a progrm that many people want to see, and is available for most microcomputers. (VisiCalc is also ideal for many library administrative functions.) It comes with a good tutorial to assist patrons who want to explore it on their own. Local vendors who are familiar with the program may be willing to give lectures or group demonstrations at the library. Many variations of VisiCalc are now on the market, including SuperCalc. (One writer, apparently amused by the proliferation, suggested InvisiCalc, a spreadsheet with a blank screen that anticipates your needs!)

Software for Children

Children and beginners are very open to suggestion regarding "What should I do next?" A general rule is to keep their abilities in focus. For example, most children do not type well, if at all. A preschooler will not be able to cope with a text-oriented program, but may do well with one requiring only the discrimination between objects, whether letters, shapes or colors. Although a few good programs for this category exist (e.g., Preschool IQ Builder), they are among the hardest to find.

If the library plans a cooperative venture with a local elementary school, a variety of programs to complement current classroom subjects will be needed. Programs for math, spelling and reading should be available for various age levels. As might be expected, some children will stick with one or two programs while others will explore the entire collection.

A number of programs for children are listed in the section on good programs for libraries, at the end of this chapter.

Entertainment

This area includes instructional and traditional games, such as computer chess, checkers, etc. Arcade games—games that are very fast-paced and visual—are not recommended. Many educational games are quite entertaining, and there are plenty of popular traditional games available on computer. Since computer games represent the bulk of micro software available today, they are discussed at length here. Examples are listed in the section on good programs for libraries, at the end of this chapter.

Computer Games: A Simple Introduction

Since so many people find the ordinary use of a microcomputer entertaining, it is very difficult to draw hard and fast distinctions between "games" and other types of activities. It is possible to distinguish between arcade, adventure, strategy, simulation and fantasy games. Games also come in three varieties—"hires" (high resolution graphics), "lores" (low resolution graphics) or text, which is to say 100% text and no graphics at all.

Arcade games include Pac Man, Snack Attack, Space Invaders, etc. Players concentrate on increasing their scores. "Just one more game!" is often the cry. Instant feedback rivets one's eyes to the screen. The greatest appreciable benefit of these fast-paced, high resolution games is improvement of motor skills (hand-eye coordination). However, they present all sorts of problems for public libraries. They are expensive, trendy and tend to promote loitering and noise. Most important, entertainment of this sort is not the primary objective of a library public access computer.

There are many high resolution graphics games that are not arcade in nature. These usually provide practice in logical thinking, following directions and color recognition. They are not "sudden death" games, which would defeat their purpose, but open-ended.

Children may play until tired or bored. Low resolution graphics games are most often elementary in nature but not always. Some are of the "hand-eye" coordination variety but they are less addicting than the hires.

The text games are the best for libraries (or perhaps for any educational institution), since they promote reading, which is our stock in trade. The pure text game simply presents line after line of text to the learner/player, requiring responses. Usually, these games are dominated by puzzle-solving activities. Quiz text games ask a series of timed or untimed questions. Players are scored according to the speed and accuracy of the answers. These games can be fun and educational.

Ground Rules for Games

The following criteria can be used for selecting computer games:

1. Have a *variety* of games to meet different preferences, skill levels and ages.

2. Select games carefully, concentrating upon text and lower resolution graphics games, which force children (or adults) to read as they go along.

3. Keep in mind that many hundreds of truly educational games exist. The Minnesota Educational Computing Consortium (MECC) and Softswap programs, described later in this chapter, can form the basis of a good collection for teaching Roman numerals, the coordinate system, logical thinking and arithmetic. These should be cataloged and described and the list made available to parents, children or anyone who wants it.

4. Be wary of games that require long periods of time to play (days or weeks), or stress that these should be considered for demonstration purposes only.

GUIDELINES FOR SOFTWARE SELECTION: A PROCESS

No one can hope to keep up with every piece of software entering the market, and no one should attempt to do so when choosing software for public access. Rather, your goals should be to ensure that the software collection fills the basic requirements of the library population, to make sure that it isn't defective and to be certain that all programs allow for the fullest and most satisfactory use of the equipment.

A process for selecting software is suggested below. Many of the steps can and probably should be pursued at the same time or in any order that works for those involved. Ideally, the entire staff will take an interest in finding new software.

Step One: Learn about the Product

It is important to become familiar with the technical aspects of software—the terms, the way in which it operates and what makes it good or bad. Reading about software can give you some of the basics, but the best, and quickest, results will come from using and experimenting with programs *on a regular basis*. This is a concept both librarians and patrons should keep in mind.

Step Two: Identify the Budget

It is said that software is the most expensive part of the computer, since it costs far more in the long run than the hardware. Determine how much of a budget you have as soon as possible. Just how much money should (or can) be spent on software will vary greatly depending on the institution, how the project is viewed by those who make budgetary decisions and so forth.

There is no point in buying a machine for several thousand dollars unless you intend to support it with adequate programming. Further, budget requests are more easily justified by the submission of concrete items for purchase. If you must fight for a software budget, keep in mind that some of the more expensive software packages can be justified by their many uses and wide appeal. Also, since the project must begin from the ground up, it may be necessary to spend more the first year than for subsequent years.

A bare bones public access system will require at least a $1500 investment in software to start. This will include a word processing package, data base management system, spreadsheet, BASIC programming package, elementary, middle and high school CAI, games and keyboard or starter programs. If additional money is available, other areas can be added, such as accounting, language packages, etc. At least $500 per year (preferably $1000) should be allocated for additional acquisitions.

Step Three: Know Your Users

As with hardware selection, when choosing software you must ask: Who will be using the computer and what for? This includes determining what age groups are going to use the computer: adult, college, high school, elementary, preschool, etc. Establishing a formal selection policy delineating your goals, objectives, areas of selection, etc., will also make a great tool for periodic review.

At this point it would be good to get input from all of the professional staff, at least. A brainstorming session is not out of the question, to clearly define the groups that the library wishes to serve. If a library has the space and the money, computers may end up in both the adult and juvenile rooms, and software selection will be pursued for different groups by separate staff. They should confer periodically, however.

Step Four: Know What Programs Are Available

Given the profusion of computer programs in the industry, this really means: Know what programs are available for your library's equipment and applications. Start by reading various computer magazines, browsing through catalogs and talking with patrons and with other librarians. Perhaps the best source of organized data about software is a software directory. It is a good idea to have one handy for your particular machine. Some volumes have reviews, others have only title and ordering information. A number of basic information sources are listed later in this chapter (see also the bibliography at the end of this book).

Step Five: Review and Preview

Important, expensive programs are often reviewed in the literature, and reviews should be checked. Word processing systems, data base management systems and the like, should be investigated and previewed. Seeing a program operate before purchase is important, but very difficult to do. Join a library users group (LUG) if possible, since such groups demonstrate software at regular meetings. Form such a group if one does not exist locally and ask vendors to participate as well. (See the discussion on library users groups in Chapter 6.) A few computer stores will allow you to preview programs before buying, but they are hard to find. You might want to use a software evaluation form, such as the one shown in Figure 3.1, for reviewing each program

Step Six: Establish Selection Criteria

The selection criteria for reviewing a software program could go on forever, but the most important questions to ask, and those most possible to check on, are listed below.

Is the software compatible with your micro? It may sound simple, but make sure Apple software is purchased for Apple computers and so on. Some versions of software will work on one model and not on a later one. Different pieces of software often require different amounts of memory. If the library computer did not come equipped with the maximum memory, some programs will not work. Be certain that you have enough memory to support the programs you want to buy. Also, if you are considering some of the more expensive word processing programs, make sure that your micro has the appropriate 80-column card, printer or other required hardware. It is vital to check on all of these details *before* you make your purchase, since most software cannot be returned.

Does it fit into the scheme of service? In short, does the software do a specific thing which is lacking in the collection or which patrons have been requesting? If the software does not fit into some area of service, think twice before buying it.

Is it bug free? Software errors can waste a great deal of time, not to mention money. Microcomputer club software libraries, which contain public domain programs, are perhaps the worst offenders. Ninety percent of all public domain software is simply programming that people have written and circulate for free. Consequently, it can contain bugs that people haven't bothered to correct. Nonetheless, public domain software is a valuable source of inexpensive and often innovative programming for a library. Just be sure to check it thoroughly with club members, other libraries or anyone else who may be familiar with it.

Commercial software is not always bug free either, and this becomes particularly important with some of the expensive programs. Unfortunately, if you purchase a com-

Figure 3.1: North-Pulaski Software Review Form

SOFTWARE REVIEW FORM TODAY'S DATE _____ 19____

1. NAME OF PROGRAM _____
   MANUFACTURER _____ VERSION _____
   REVIEWER _____

2. CATEGORY _____ EDUCATION _____ RECREATION _____ BUSINESS
   _____ ADMINISTRATIVE _____ SCIENTIFIC _____ STATISTICAL _____
   OTHER (PLEASE SPECIFY) _____

3. GRADE OR EDUCATION LEVEL _____ COLLEGE _____ ELEMENTARY (K-3)
   _____ ELEMENTARY (CIRCLE ONE OR MORE) 4 5 6 7 8
   _____ HIGH SCHOOL (CIRCLE ONE OR MORE) 9 10 11 12

4. IS THIS PROGRAM OF SPECIAL INTEREST TO ANY PARTICULAR GROUP?
   _____ HANDICAPPED _____ SENIOR CITIZENS _____ GED _____ ESL
   _____ OTHER (PLEASE SPECIFY) _____
   _____
   _____
   _____

5. WHAT IS THE PURPOSE OF THE PROGRAM? (BRIEF DESCRIPTION): _____
   _____ CONTINUE ON BACK OF FORM

6. WHAT LANGUAGE? _____ INTEGER _____ FLOATING POINT _____
   _____ OTHER (PLEASE SPECIFY) _____

7. HOW WELL DOES IT ACHIEVE ITS PURPOSE?

8. DOES IT USE ANY SPECIAL GRAPHICS, ETC.?

9. DOES IT USE OR NEED A _____ PRINTER _____ MODEM _____ TWO DRIVES
   MEMORY NEEDED _____ K

10. OTHER GENERAL COMMENTS OR THOUGHTS ABOUT THIS PROGRAM? _____
    _____
    _____
    _____
    _____

                                       (CONTINUE ON BACK OF FORM)

mercial program with bugs in it, you are often stuck with it. However, some companies have begun to respond to complaints about their products, so it is worthwhile to contact the manufacturer if your software is defective.

Is it interactive? Observing this criterion might improve the software more than anything else. If the program just turns pages of text on the screen, why tie up the computer with something that could be done just as well with a book?

Is it well-documented? Some programs have self-contained documentation, i.e., the instructions are displayed as part of the program. This type of documentation is best because it cannot be lost unless the disk is destroyed. However, if there are insufficient instructions in the program, make sure that clear and easy-to-follow printed instructions are included.

Complicated or advanced programs will sometimes have a tutorial to assist users, and these too may be part of the actual program or included in the accompanying manual. Programs with tutorials are especially helpful for a public library because they will assist patrons who are expecting a great deal of individual attention.

Is it a good value? High price does not necessarily mean high quality, and an advertiser's claim that a program is "powerful" can mean nothing. Many very inexpensive (even free) programs are goldmines. Some very expensive programs will turn out to be duds.

Can it be returned? This is a sticky issue. Few manufacturers are willing to return money. We all seem to be suffering because of the underground traffic in pirated software. A software manufacturer who will send merchandise on approval should be patronized in good faith. *Never* keep a copy of something that has been returned.

Is there a backup provision? Many manufacturers allow the purchaser to make a backup copy of the program, as long as it is not given to anyone else. Some companies will provide a backup copy for a modest fee of $5 or so. Others, such as Microlab, provide an extended warranty and two copies of the program in order to prevent downtime from the inevitable "bomb." This is a good idea for a major expensive program.

Is it instructionally sound? This is an important criterion for choosing educational software. Programs should be factual and do a good job of teaching. If a program covers a subject area in which the reviewer is an expert, a quick check of the material should be made. If an error pops up, the program is probably not up to standards.*

---

* Ann Lathrop listed ten reasons for automatically rejecting a program in *Educational Computer* (September/October 1982). These ten reasons—primarily regarding educational programs—range from incompatibility to "embarrassing the student." They are helpful as guidelines, although not all can be followed absolutely.

SOFTWARE INFORMATION SOURCES

Software reviews and descriptions are important selection tools, and are not always easy to find. The best sources for this type of information are computer periodicals, directories and data bases. There are now hundreds of computer magazines, and new directories and data bases become available regularly. The information sources listed below are by no means exhaustive, but they do represent publications that should be of interest to public access librarians. (See Appendix E for addresses of the periodicals listed.) Be wary of reviews that provide *only* descriptions, not evaluations. These are sometimes taken directly from the sales literature provided by the manufacturer.

Periodicals

Among the computer magazines, *Small Computers In Libraries, Educational Computer, Classroom Computer Learning* and *Software Review* are aimed specifically at educators and librarians.

Microcomputer Index is a subject index to nearly 40 journals, including *Byte, Creative Computing, Personal Computing, Classroom Computer Learning* and *Softalk.* Each issue contains abstracts. The magazine is published bimonthly by Microcomputer Information Services. It is also available online through Dialog Information Services and its lower-cost evening version, Knowledge Index.

An irregular feature of the American Library Association (ALA) publication *Booklist* is microcomputer software reviews for school and public libraries. Only recommended software is listed. The October 1, 1981 issue contained 20 "Evaluation Criteria for Microcomputer Software." The criteria are geared toward educational programs and ask questions such as "Does the program allow the student to build on already developed skills?"

Directories and Data Bases

Directories and catalogs of software for specific computers are becoming more widespread and better organized. The examples listed below are good for staff or public use; many more are available.

DataPro Research Corp. (1805 Underwood Blvd., Delran, NJ 08075) has developed an impressive set of directories to aid anyone searching for microcomputer hardware or software. Included are special sections on clubs, vendors, printers, disk drives, memory and more. These directories are in looseleaf format and are frequently updated. One big drawback for small libraries is the price: $475 for the *Directory of Microcomputer Software.* Other specific titles include *Directory of Small Computers* and *Management of Small Computers.*

Digest of Software Reviews provides abstracts of software reviews from more than 70 journals. It is published four times each year with 50 software packages covered in each issue. Published by: The Digest of Software Reviews, 1341 Bulldog Lane, Suite C9, Fresno, CA 93710.

International Software Database, available online through the Dialog Knowledge Index, lists more than 6500 pieces of software. Listings include software descriptions, date of release, price, vendor information, and other data.

MicroSIFT is a project of the Northwest Regional Education Laboratory. While the MicroSIFT newsletter is no longer published, the courseware descriptions that are generated are still available through journals. They are also available through Resources In Computer Education (RICE), described below.

The *Online Micro-software Guide and Directory* describes more than 700 packages of software including hardware requirements, language, operating systems, etc. It contains sections on many other aspects of computer operation, including software problems to be aware of, and has a resource section and an index. Published by Online, Inc., 11 Tannery Lane, Weston, CT 06883.

Resources in Computer Education (RICE) is a computer data base available online through Bibliographic Retrieval Services (BRS). It is not available on BRS After Dark. RICE contains some 2000 microcomputer entries, describing and evaluating courseware for elementary and secondary education. Details and local access points can be obtained from: Northwest Regional Educational Laboratory, 300 S.W. Sixth Ave., Portland, OR 97204.

The *Software Vendor Directory* contains more than 1800 microcomputer software vendors and 123 hardware vendors. It lists 12,300 software products in 300 categories. Published by: Micro-Software Services, Inc., Box 482, Nyack, NY 10960.

WHERE TO FIND IT TO BUY IT

Software is now sold just about everywhere, including the street corner (how legally is another matter!). Librarians thus have a number of options available for procuring software, including software vendors, public domain clubs and company donations.

Software Vendors

The most obvious place to look for software is in the local computer store, but it is not necessarily the best place. A computer store is a good place to get information on a particular piece of software, but always compare store prices with catalog prices, which are often discounted. Also keep in mind that much software is available *only* through mail-order.

The best policy is to find a good library vendor (of books, audiovisual supplies, etc.) who also deals in software. However, when ordering through a library vendor, you must know exactly what you want. Often, library vendor software catalogs just list titles and prices, without descriptions.

General purpose and specialized software houses are listed in Appendix C. These sell software of interest to librarians planning a public access computer project. Simply write to the company for a catalog. One handy guide, for the public as well as for professional research, is the *Software Publishers' Catalogs Annual* ($97.50). It contains software publishers' catalogs on microfiche, and is published annually by Meckler Publishing, 520 Riverside Ave., Westport, CT 06880.

Public Domain Club Libraries

Much software can be obtained free through clubs and user groups.* However, as mentioned previously, there can be problems. Programs available through clubs sometimes must be debugged and categorized before they can be used by the public, a time-consuming procedure. Be wary of cluttering up the collection with many small, worthless programs—they will make the job of compiling a subject guide to the collection that much more difficult. Also, some club exchanges will not replace defective diskettes. Many clubs have listings in computer journals (see Appendix E), including each issue of *Computer Shopper*.

Company Donations

You may succeed in obtaining free software by sending letters to a number of software companies. Simply describe the operation, emphasizing that it is for the public, explain that the library is unable to buy all the software it needs. Many companies will be pleased to have their software demonstrated or used by patrons, hoping, of course, that patrons will then go out and purchase a copy.

Three things should be emphasized in your request:

1. No one is allowed to copy any programs under copyright at the library. If patrons sign some type of agreement stating that they will not reproduce or pirate library-owned programs for their personal use, send a copy along.

2. The software donors will probably get more publicity from the contribution than it will cost them. Emphasize that many people will become aware of the program, but because library computer time is limited, few will be able to use it properly without purchasing it.

3. The library is tax-exempt and contributions are deductible.

Software Packages

One good way to stock up on many simple, introductory programs, quite suitable for beginners and younger users, is to purchase a package. Software purchased in bulk can often be a bargain. The items listed below are meant only as examples of what is available. New packages appear regularly.

---

*"How to Get Free Software," *Popular Computing* (December 1983), lists some 15 different locations for public domain software.

American Software Publishing Co. produces *Applefreeloader: Guide to Public Domain Software for Apple Computers,* an extensive list of software for the Apple. The catalog includes a listing of clubs and user groups. The company also offers a great public domain collection, containing 2500 programs of all descriptions, grouped by subject (e.g., adventure, home, utilities, games, etc.), for only $500. Contact: American Software Publishing Co., Box 57221, Washington, DC 20037.

Appleware has produced an excellent introductory package of 540 public domain programs for only $389. Contact: Appleware Inc., 6400 Hayes St., Hollywood, FL 33024.

Fisher Scientific Co. offers the Commodore Educational Software Package, containing 656 public domain programs, for $450. The programs include computer science, history, French, geography, math and games, and range from primary school to college level. Contact: Fisher Scientific Co., Educational Materials Division, 4901 W. LeMoyne Street, Chicago, IL 60651.

The CP/M User's Group has about 100 diskettes of public domain software. For current information contact: CP/M User's Group, 345 E. 86th St., New York, NY 10028.

The Folklife Terminal Club offers more than 5000 public domain programs in over 25 categories for the Commodore PET, Commodore VIC and the Commodore CBM. A "Catalog Disk" has a listing of all available programs. Contact: Folklife Club, Box 2222, Mt. Vernon, NY 10551.

The Minnesota Educational Computing Consortium (MECC) has produced an excellent set of microcomputer diskettes for elementary, middle and high school use. Diskettes are sold separately and are on subjects such as mathematics, science, language arts and social studies. By purchasing a number of these disks, which average $40 each, you can make a good, basic education package. The programs are for Apple II or Atari micros. Contact: MECC Distribution Center, 2520 Broadway Dr., St. Paul, MN 55113.

The San Mateo County Office of Education and Computer-Using Educators jointly offer Softswap, which consists of general purpose software, mostly educational in nature. Local participants can walk in and copy the software free. If ordered through the mail, each disk is $10, with from six to 25 programs on a disk. If an original program is "swapped," the Softswap diskette is free. Contact: Softswap, SMERC Library, San Mateo County Office of Education, 333 Main St., Redwood City, CA 94063.

ORGANIZING AND MAINTAINING THE SOFTWARE COLLECTION

Your software collection will be more easily managed if the following rules are observed.

1. Do not create a filing system that is so complicated that it takes a great deal of time to maintain, or is unclear to patrons and staff.

2. There should be a unique place and number for each diskette.

3. It should be easy to keep track of what software is in use at any given time.

4. There should be limited and controlled access to the software area.

5. Documentation should be stored with the diskettes whenever possible.

Filing

A simple filing system will work well for most library software collections. At North-Pulaski, diskettes are numbered sequentially as they are acquired, and filed by acquisition number. Titles of the programs on each diskette are filed alphabetically with the corresponding file number. This makes it easy to find individual programs.

Try to avoid gimmicks such as box-type systems. They are attractive-looking, but when used, diskettes become jumbled up and difficult to find.

One good system is to store diskettes in two-up plastic sheets or pages, which can be kept in binders. These provide an individual slot for each diskette and allow easy access to holdings.

Cataloging Software

In most cases, it is not necessary to catalog software, unless the library wants software to be listed as part of the overall collection. If you intend to catalog software, *Guidelines for Cataloging Microcomputer Software, 1982* (compiled by the Wisconsin Educational Media Association) is a handy booklet available for only $2. It is illustrated with examples of catalog cards. Available from: Don Jorgenson, McKinley Instructional Service Center, 1010 Huron St., Manitowoc, WI 54220. Another publication is *A Manual of AACR2 Examples for Microcomputer Software and Video Games*. It costs $10 and is a 75-page manual including 25 examples for various micros. Available from: Soldier Creek Press, 642 S. Hunt St., Lake Crystal, MN 56055.

Software Wall Chart

If you have several hundred or more programs in your collection, you can use a data base program, such as Master Catalog or Data Factory, to produce a laminated Software Wall Chart (see Figure 3.2). (See Chapter 7 for how to produce a wall chart.) List all important or interesting programs with corresponding disk numbers, and post the chart in the library for patrons to scan. It should save everyone a great deal of time. It also partly answers the perennial question, "What will the computer do?", since it is in many ways a list of applications.

Figure 3.2: Portion of North-Pulaski Software Wall Chart

```
049 I  I DARE YOU
056    ICBM: COORDINATE SYSTEM: MECC
071 A  IMPOSSIBLE FIGURE (HIRES DRAWINGS
          THAT DEFIES LAWS OF PERSPECTIVE)
214 I  INTERACTIVE BASEBALL
037 I  INTERCEPT
211 A  INTEREST
000    INTRODUCTION TO THE MICROCOMPUTER
027 A  INVESTMENTS
000    INVOICE FACTORY (BUSINESS)
046    JOUST (ANCIENT JOUSTING)
034 I  KATO
022    KEYBOARD FOR THE APPLE
       KNOW YOUR APPLE (INTRODUCTION)
021 I  KIDSTUFF
011 I  KISS TRIVIA
041 A  KLINGON CAPTURE
072 A  LAF ISLAND (SURVIVAL SIMULATION):
          SOFTSWAP
216 I  LANDER-S
052    LANGUAGE ARTS (ELEM, V.2): MECC
040 I  LASER BOMB  (TWO PLAYERS NEEDED)
041 I  LASER CANNON
035 A  LAST PAYMENT ON A LOAN
202 A  LATITUDE/LONGITUDE FINDER
000    LEARNING SYSTEM (CREATE A QUIZ, ETC)
029 A  LEASES I
021 I  LEGACY (MULTIPLICATION GAME)
122    LEGIONNAIRE (ANCIENT BATTLE GAME)
044 A  LEM (LUNAR LANDING)
053    LEMONADE (MANAGEMENT GAME): MECC
121    LIBRARY SKILLS: BARTLETT'S
117    LIBRARY SKILLS: DICTIONARY
```

Back Up

In general, all valuable diskettes should be backed up before use and stored in a safe place, preferably a remote location. However, it should never take more than 24 hours to replace a diskette.

Always back up programs before making them available for public access. Most programs can be backed up with a simple copy program (which is often provided with the machine). Others may require more sophisticated copy programs. For programs that can't be copied, the library must rely on warranty or backup provisions from the vendor.

Weeding the Collection

Most software collections require minimal weeding. Only a few libraries will be able to buy enough software to make this necessary. However, the larger the collection becomes, the more difficult and expensive it is to maintain. Older programs, primarily those that have been replaced by better, more recent ones, should be put to rest. The diskette can usually be put back into service as a backup or used to copy programs in the public domain.

GOOD PROGRAMS FOR PUBLIC LIBRARIES

The following programs have worked well for public access micro projects. Consider them only examples and do not be concerned if a favorite program is not among them—not all programs could be listed. All information is as of early 1984. New software appears almost daily, and vendors should be contacted for the most up-to-date information. Addresses for the software companies listed below are given in Appendix C.

Atariwriter is a word processing system, described on page 34. Micro: Atari. Vendor: Regional Atari representatives ($99.95).

Calico library skills programs, described on page 32, are $29.95 each (a $5 sample diskette available).

Classic Library Programs include 12 CAI library skills programs, described on page 32. Micros: Apple, Commodore PET, Commodore 64. Vendor: Right On Programs ($18 per program).

CompuRead 3.0 is a learning skills program that makes very effective use of computer technology. Letters, numbers and sentences flash across the screen at a user-defined pace. Micro: Apple. Vendor: Edu-Ware Services, Inc. ($29.95).

CompuSpell permits up to 60 individuals to maintain a personal record of progress. Essentially "drill and practice," the program is geared to grades 4 through 8, plus adult/secretarial level. Micro: Apple. Vendor: Edu-Ware Services, Inc. ($29.95 for system disk; $19.95 for each of six levels.).

The Data Factory is a data base management system, described on page 33. Micros: Apple, IBM PC. Vendor: Microlab ($300).

Facemaker is for children from ages 4 to 12. This program quickly builds the child's confidence at the keyboard by presenting an entertaining way to create the computer counterpart of the toy Mr. Potato Head. From a selection displayed on the screen, a face is shaped and then reshaped from combinations of noses, mouths, eyes, etc. At any point, the child may "program" the face to perform a series of winks, smiles, ear wiggles, etc. Micros: Apple, Atari, Commodore 64. Vendor: Spinnaker Software Corp. ($34.95).

FCM—Filing, Cataloging and Mailing (Formerly First Class Mail)—is a data base management system, described on page 33. Micros: Apple ($99.95), Commodore 64 ($49.95), IBM PC ($124.95). Vendor: Continental Software.

Gertrude's Secrets and **Gertrude's Puzzles** are two similar programs which help the child learn colors, shapes and logical thinking, while promoting reading. Although aimed at ages 4 to 9, adults will also enjoy it. Gertrude zips through the rooms of her house picking up objects and transporting them from place to place. Children can play for long or short periods. *Requires color.* Micro: Apple. Vendor: The Learning Co. ($44.95 each).

Haunted House is an example of a good game that improves and encourages reading. It is one of the most popular programs at North-Pulaski, and is for elementary through adult levels. The computer constructs a different 24-room mansion in each game. The only way out, a secret passage, must be found by "midnight" or the player will be stuck in the dungeon forever. Micro: Apple. Vendor: Compuware ($11.95).

Home Accountant is a complete home accounting package. This program is for demonstration purposes, since it requires monthly use to perform functions on a continuing basis. It can be used with an 80-column printer (other accounting packages usually require more). Micros: Apple, Atari, Commodore 64 ($74.95), IBM PC ($150). Vendor: Continental Software.

Hurkle (and other coordinate grid games) have the player explore the grid by entering different coordinates, searching for little "Hurkle." Micro: Apple. Vendor: MECC (on the Elementary Volume 1 Math diskette, $45).

Keyboard programs to introduce novices to the computer are available for several different machines. Ask your local dealer for prices.

Know Your Apple ($34.95) and **Know Your Apple IIe** ($24.95) teach children the fundamentals of the Apple computer. Vendor: Muse Software.

LOGO is a programming language available for most major microcomputers. It is especially suited for preschool users, but can be used by any age level. Check appropriate catalogs for prices for different models.

Magic Spells is an adventure in spelling. Children meet the "Spelling Demon," and unscramble words to find a treasure. Micro: Apple. Vendor: The Learning Co. ($34.95).

MasterType: The Typing Instruction Game is a high resolution instructional package. Micros: Apple, Atari, Commodore 64 ($39.95), IBM PC ($49.95). Vendor: Scarborough Systems.

Microzine is an online version of a magazine for ages 10 and up. Micros: Apple. Vendor: Scholastic, Inc. ($39.95 per issue; six issues per year).

Mystery House (Apple $19.95) and **Princess and the Wizard** (Apple, Atari, Commodore 64, $29.95) are high resolution graphics games that require thought and concentration to work through the maze of puzzles. Beginners should start with **Mission Asteroid** (Apple, Atari, $19.95), a simple version meant to instruct those who have not played such games before. Other games in the series include **Cranston Manor** ($29.95) and **Ulysses and the Golden Fleece** (Apple, Atari, IBM, $32.95), and **The Dark Crystal** (Apple, Atari, IBM, $37.95). Vendor: Sierra On-Line Inc.

The New Step by Step is an excellent multimedia BASIC tutorial for grades 7 and up. Micros: Apple, Atari ($99.95), Commodore PET ($59.95). Vendor: Program Design, Inc.

Odell Lake and **Odell Woods** both require some imagination. The student takes the role of either a fish or some other animal (depending upon the ecosystem) and attempts to survive in a simulated food chain. Micro: Apple. Vendor: MECC (both available on the Elementary Volume 4 Math and Science diskette, $15).

Oregon Trail is a text management game. To get to Oregon, the "pioneer" must manage a wagon train, food and supplies, stop at forts along the way, and deal with unfriendly types ("Indians" are not mentioned, by the way). The software comes with a simple, reproducible printed worksheet. This has been a tremendously popular game for elementary grades and up in some libraries. The game may be a bit less popular in the Western states, where the incentive to get to Oregon may not be as strong! Micros: Apple, Atari, TRS-80. Vendor: Softswap ($10, or free).

Pie Writer (Pie 2.2) is a word processing system, described on page 34. Micros: Apple ($149), IBM PC ($199.95). Vendor: Hayden Book Co.

PLATO modules are based on the highly successful and popular PLATO learning system. Units include French, German, Spanish, physics, fractions, computer literacy and others. Micros: Apple, Atari, Texas Instruments. Vendor: Control Data Publishing Co. ($60 each; physics, $70).

Preschool I.Q. Builder permits the parent (in most cases) to choose the level of involvement, including shape recognition and letter differentiation. The child must only press one of two keys to participate. Vendor: P.D.Q. Software ($23.95).

Primer teaches the fundamentals of the IBM personal computer. This is essentially a keyboard program. Micro: IBM. Vendor: Computer Systems Research, Inc. ($210).

Screenwriter II is a word processing program, described on page 34. Micro: Apple. Vendor: Sierra On-Line, Inc. ($129.95).

Startrek is still one of the preeminently popular computer games around and is available in many versions through various manufacturers. This is not a fast arcade game; strategy is required. Available through many vendors for numerous computers.

Story Machine lets children from ages 5 to 7 write stories using a vocabulary supplied by the computer. The story is then animated on the screen. Micros: Apple, Atari, IBM PC ($39.95), Commodore 64 ($34.95). Vendor: Spinnaker Software Corp.

SuperCalc is a spreadsheet, described on page 34. Micros: Apple, IBM PC. Vendor: Sorcim Corp. ($195).

Three Mile Island is a simulation game that makes participants regulate a nuclear power plant, including water pressure and steam. The object is to operate the plant profitably without "melting down." This is a good simulation program for grades 5 and up. It is difficult to play without color. Micro: Apple. Vendor: Muse Software ($39.95).

Tic-Tac-Facts is a math review game with six levels of difficulty for grades 1 through 8. Players must answer a series of math exercises correctly in order to place an "X" or "O" on the board. Micro: Commodore VIC 20. Vendor: Scholastic, Inc. ($9.95).

Type Attack has 39 prepared lessons and 60 lessons which may be defined by the user, both with sound effects and graphics. Micro: Apple. Vendor: Sirius Software ($39.95).

Typing Tutor II is an instructional program. As soon as the typing test is finished. instant results, including an analysis of typing skills and keys most often missed, are flashed on the screen. Exercises for practicing certain keys are also provided. Up to 60 students may keep their scores recorded on the master diskette. Micro: Apple. Vendor: Microsoft Corp. ($24.95).

Valdez is an imaginative, but difficult, game. The "captain" of the "Valdez"—the player—struggles to take the tanker and cargo up a foggy seaway. Such factors as current, rudder control and engineer speed must be calculated. Micro: Apple. Vendor: DynaComp ($23.95).

VisiCalc is an analyzing and forecasting spreadsheet program, described on page 34. Micros: Apple, IBM PC, Commodore 8032 and 8096. Vendor: Distributed through most dealers ($250).

Wizardry is probably the best of the dungeon games. Players see their actions through high resolution graphics, and are also given a constantly updated set of game parameters in the corner of the screen. Such games, sometimes referred to as "Computer Dungeons and Dragons," can be used in a number of ways, including tournaments or demonstrations. If only one or two microcomputers are available, they may be taken over by the dungeon set. Micro: Apple. Vendor: Sir-Tech Software, Inc. ($49.95).

WordStar is a word processing package, described on page 34. Micros: Apple, IBM PC. Vendor: MicroPro International Corp. ($495).

Zork I, II and III are adventure text games that require a great deal of reading. The player is in a world of cyclops, thieves and trolls. Micros: Apple, Atari, IBM PC. Vendor: Infocom Software ($39.95).

4

Managing the Project

This chapter discusses some of the management considerations that must be addressed when introducing a public access micro into the library. Three major areas are covered: the computer itself, in terms of its location, security and maintenance; staff and partron training; and issues of overall service management. The emphasis is on operating a personal computer center that is complementary to other library services, not one that detracts, or is divorced, from them.

CHOOSING A LOCATION

Three basic considerations should be kept in mind when deciding on the physical location for hardware and software. The first is noise from both equipment and users. Most printers operate more noisily than can be tolerated in a public reading area. Also, many people, especially children, naturally become loud when enjoying themselves. If it is not careful, the library could quickly end up as another arcade (even if it doesn't offer arcade games) as patrons "discover" the microcomputer.

Next, consider where the software will be kept and who on the staff will control its distribution. (The task of taking library cards and giving out diskettes isn't such a bad job, because it means talking with patrons on a regular basis. That may keep librarians abreast of patron needs and improve software selection.) The software should be distributed by someone in a central spot (reference or circulation desk); patrons should not have to walk great distances through the library.

It's important to have a way to close the micro area off when the responsible personnel are unavailable. Ideally, the equipment should be in a separate room that can be locked.

If possible, have at least two machines at any one location or building. Having both machines the same brand (if not model) may reduce software costs and require fewer training sessions.

Obviously, wherever the hardware is put, adequate outlets and wiring will be needed, along with proper lighting, furniture[1] and moderate room temperature. Any kind of online operation will also require a telephone nearby. The final consideration, and perhaps the most important, is security.

SECURITY

The first rule for ensuring the security of the public microcomputer is: *It should not be visible from the street!* Since thieves will steal the coins from library copy machines, old typewriters and fiche readers, just imagine their excitement when they find out that the library has a microcomputer!

There are many kinds of thieves. There is the casual thief, who will steal something only if it's easy to do so, and the professional burglar, who will stop at nothing. Stopping the casual thief is the easiest. This sort often includes the patron who absconds with a circuit board when no one is looking. There are simple devices for stopping this type of offender.

At the very least, install anchor pads under the computer, printer, drives and monitor. Better yet, install a locking mechanism that will keep fingers on the outside of the computer where they belong.

One of the best security devices for the Apple is the Station II: Apple Support System, which also keeps all unsightly cords out of reach. This is also one of the most reasonably priced units ($129 in early 1984). If not available locally, it can be obtained through Midwest Visual Equipment Co. (6500 N. Hamlin Ave., Chicago, IL 60645). Also, steel cable security devices, called the Apple Locker, are available from Tele-Terminals (7008 Northland Dr., Minneapolis, MN 55428).

The Anchor Pad computer security system, which can be used with any micro, guards monitor, drives and computer and allows the machine to be rotated 360 degrees. The approximate retail price in early 1984 was $445. It is available from Anchor Pad International, Inc. (3224 Thatcher Ave., Marina Del Rey, CA 90292). Tec-Mart, Inc. (Box 297, Hinsdale, IL 60521) sells the L1D—an acrylic protective enclosure—for the Apple, IBM PC and TRS-80 micros. In early 1984, prices ranged from $145 to $200.

A security system consisting of electronic surveillance, dogs and security guards will help, but nothing affords complete protection against the determined professional criminal. Just take the approach that some protection is better than none. If real electronic surveillance is not possible, post authentic-looking warning stickers or inexpensive surveillance cameras to make someone think twice. If one small room is used for the computer room or as an overnight storage area, it should be easy to make it secure.

The Anchor Pad computer security system has a 360° swivel feature. It locks the disk drives, monitor and computer into place. Courtesy of Anchor Pad International.

CARING FOR THE EQUIPMENT

Proper care of a computer differs from proper security. A computer is a very expensive and valuable tool. Any time it is not operating (even temporarily) is value lost. The suggestions below are only a starting point for proper care. Preventive maintenance can help to save hours or days of downtime.

To begin with, *carefully read the manuals that came with the computer*; they will answer many questions. It's advisable to hide a set of manuals so that only the staff dealing with the microcomputer has access to them: It's incredible how fast manuals disappear. Next, ground all electrical cords if possible.

Things to Avoid

The following recommendations are very general and can apply to most microcomputers using disk drives and printers. Consult the microcomputer manual for more details.

1. Liquids. Do not allow any liquids in the computer area. Accidental spillage could destroy the machine. Keep the computer away from condensation, oil and chemical fumes.

2. Dirt. Dirt can accumulate in the drives and ruin data. Do not smoke in the computer area, as drives do not like smoke. Drives should be cleaned regularly with the recommended solvents and materials (usually, cleaning diskettes).

3. Heat. See that the heat in the room is fairly constant and within the guidelines in the manuals. Do not restrict the airflow around the machine by covering up any vents, etc. If the computer contains more than a few circuit boards, some overheating may occur. Small fans, specifically designed for use with home computers, are available through many sources. They will effectively lengthen the life of computer components by lowering their temperatures.

4. Jarring. The computer (and especially the printer) should be positioned on a stable surface to prevent undue vibration or movement. Never allow any of the equipment to be dropped or roughly handled.

Handling Diskettes

The following recommendations pertain to any type of diskette.

1. Don't stack, bend, fold or squeeze them!

2. To avoid dust buildup, keep diskettes in their paper jackets when not in use.

3. Avoid extreme temperatures. If diskettes have been in a cold area for a long time, allow 24 hours for them to reach normal room temperature.

4. If you are labeling diskettes, write on the label *before* affixing it to the diskette.

5. Insert diskettes into drives correctly.

6. Back up all valuable programs. Store originals *away* from the computer site. Do not use the same diskette for backing up every session. If you do, it will receive all of the strain and fail abruptly.

7. Never touch the exposed surfaces of the diskette.

8. Keep diskettes away from telephones, color TVs or anything that produces electromagnetic waves. They can destroy the data on the diskettes. *Never turn the computer on or off with a diskette in the drive* as the on/off process can create a power surge or abnormality and destroy data.

9. Teach all of these things to patrons and staff.

Printer Care

Most printers do not require a lot of care, but some caution should be exercised. For instance, most letter quality printers do not stop when the paper is low or the ribbon is nearing the end. The printer will continue to print even if the paper or ribbon runs out. Always check to make sure that the supplies will meet the current printing requirements.

Someone should always be near the printer in case there is an irregularity, such as a paper jam, during operation. This is especially true in a library, where many people will be using a printer for the first time.

STAFF AND PATRON TRAINING

Once a public access operation is established, it should take no more than 5% of professional staff time to maintain, probably less. Of course, much time will be needed in the early stages of the operation, perhaps the first three to six months, to orient both staff and patrons.

Staff Training

All of the staff members who will be involved with the public access micro project should receive enough training to be able to operate the machine and to help patrons with simple questions when they get stuck. Few staff members need to be taught how to set up and operate an electronic spreadsheet, word processing or data base management program for public access work.

The equipment dealer or a local consultant may be willing to provide some training for free. If not, the library can hire a computer hobbyist from the community or perhaps have one come in on a volunteer basis. In some cases, a member of the library staff may already have enough expertise to train the others. Whichever method is chosen, the key ingredient of any public access training program is to allow enough hands-on experience for everyone, over a period of time. Time must be scheduled on a regular basis for every staff member to become familiar with the machine. In most cases, once the staff member learns the fundamentals, he or she will no longer be intimidated by the equipment.

All libraries will probably experience resistance to learning about a new technology from some staff members. In the worst case, the staff will rebel completely, leaving one or two members to shoulder the load for the whole project. However, this can be avoided by designing a training program that is enjoyable, as well as informative. The following are some suggestions for developing a training program.

1. Schedule staff members in pairs. This makes it easier and more fun for everyone. People can provide encouragement to one another and learn from others' mistakes. Check on them only if necessary, and then only to give a needed gentle push. When possible, schedule people who you know work well together.

2. Don't schedule people during times when they are badly needed by the rest of the staff. Resentment toward the program will build up if the training program interferes with ongoing library services.

3. Begin with a keyboard program. Next, have an experienced staff member sit with the trainees for the first hour, during the operation of some elementary educational programs, to give suggestions on keyboard operation and to answer questions.

4. Schedule time at the computer on a regular basis. An hour a day for 10 days per trainee is appropriate. Three one-hour sessions per week for four weeks is another good approach.

5. Staff should be encouraged to experiment and to play some of the text games and even a few high resolution graphics games. Steer clear of complicated programs such as word processing or data base management during this initial phase of training. Remember, learning to use the computer should be fun.

6. Avoid classroom-type lectures; they won't do anyone much good. They are certainly not a substitute for hands-on practice during the initial micro training sessions.

7. Get the entire staff together at least once to answer general questions. Demonstrate at least 10 *simple* programs just to answer the question, "What will the micro do?" Select programs that show off the varied capabilities of a micro.

8. If a staff member already owns a micro or has some experience with one, put him or her in charge of training and orientation. However, *do not rely exclusively on that person (or on any one person) to maintain the project.* Your program will be in trouble any time the person is out sick, goes on vacation or gets another job.

9. Distribute a glossary of terms to the staff. Include the five or six most important commands for the computer, along with definitions of the most important computer terms (hardware, software, disk drive, etc.).

10. *Do not teach programming as part of the initial training program.* Instruction can be given later on, if someone wishes to learn programming. Anyone who deals with a micro eventually learns at least some small amount of programming, but an enforced leap to this level is enough to scare off otherwise willing staff. Think users, not programmers.

11. Have a staff tournament, pitting staff trainee teams against each other. Scores can be posted weekly in the staff room.

12. Have a qualified staff member observe while beginners work with the public for the first time. Do this as soon as possible. Have the trainees explain what the equipment does and how various parts of it work. If they falter, coach them until they can manage on their own. Finally, leave trainees alone with the patrons. They will learn the most by doing, and can always get help when necessary.

Patron Training

For the most part, patrons being introduced to the microcomputer for the first time must learn the same basics as the staff. These include the following:

1. The parts of the computer, including drives, monitor and keyboard;

2. The meaning of an operating system or disk operating system;

3. The difference between hardware and software;

4. How to insert and care for diskettes;

5. How to start up or "boot" the system;

6. How to initialize a diskette (i.e., prepare it for original use);

7. How to run programs and how to abort them, using various strategies (including turning off the machine).

Computer literacy can, of course, include much more, but the library's obligation to provide assistance and training can end with the above.

Many libraries offering public access micro services require all patrons to complete a short orientation session, class, seminar or workshop prior to using the computer. The patron's library card is then stamped, entitling the patron to use the library computer. Such workshops can be scheduled weekly, biweekly or monthly. They can be designed to accommodate large or small groups, but smaller groups are preferable, since seeing and using the computer is an essential part of the training program.

Of course, some patrons will require more than one session to become comfortable with the equipment, and others may not respond well to this type of instruction. My own experience has led me to believe that only hands-on training will suffice. A half-hour keyboard program and a brief orientation are superior to any sort of group training. However, each library will have to develop a program based on its particular resources, staff availability and patron needs. Whichever method you choose, it will help to have "training sheets" available for patrons, containing a list of resources at the library and a number of recommended starter programs.

The Rolling Meadows (IL) Public Library has had a great deal of success with a patron training program.[2] Patrons must attend two workshops, one week apart. At the first workshop each patron is given some hands-on experience and a worksheet. The rules are discussed and the library staff also checks to make sure everyone has a valid library card. At the second workshop, logging on, logging off and other simple tasks are demonstrated, and patrons are given a brief test. At the end of the second workshop, patrons are registered as computer users at the library. (Both the test and worksheets are reproduced in Chapter 5.)

Another method has been used successfully at the North-Pulaski Branch Library since 1981. It is simpler, and reflects a completely hands-on approach. Patrons are first instructed in the fundamentals of disk care (i.e., "This is a diskette! Do not bend it, fold it or touch the exposed surfaces.") After this brief introduction, patrons are given a keyboard program which takes them on a tour of the computer keyboard and explains the fundamentals of operation. The keyboard program ends with a game. Afterward, patrons can continue with a series of diskettes that give progressively more advanced instruction, including programming. From this point on, patrons are encouraged to select their own diskettes from the "Software Wall Chart" (illustrated in Chapter 3).

SERVICE MANAGEMENT ISSUES

This section discusses some of the practical aspects to consider in the daily operation of the library's personal computer center. They include: conducting first-time patron interviews, scheduling appointments for computer time, how much backup assistance to provide to patrons and charging for services.

The entire operation will run much more efficiently if you identify all of the tasks that have to be performed—e.g., distribute software, orient patrons, monitor machines—and assign responsibility for them. For example, the circulation staff may distribute software, the reference staff may be best suited to conducting patron interviews or orientation, etc. Many of these decisions can be made prior to initiating the service, but adjustments may become necessary once the program actually starts.

Patron Interview

Each patron is unique and each has a different skill and interest level. Some, knowing absolutely nothing about computers, will want the library to offer a self-study course with as much personalized instruction as possible. This is neither possible nor desirable in a public library. To avoid misunderstanding, stress the idea of "self-service" in all patron interviews (and in all promotional literature). Only occasional—but important—backup support can be provided. Beyond this, patrons should be encouraged to enroll in a course elsewhere or to acquire a tutor. Information about such resources should be available at the library for patron referral.

Linda Callaghan, in discussing reference interviews with children, describes several special considerations for work with the very young.[3] Since, as we saw earlier, as many as 40% of all computer patrons are beginners with respect to hardware and software, these considerations apply equally well to many adult users.

The most important issues are:

1. Identifying the "real" subject area;

2. Determining the amount of information needed;

3. The most useful form for the information; and

4. The reading level (or here, program level) for the patron.

Before proceeding with any other information, it is best to make some effort to determine the computer literacy level of the user. In this way the library can determine if orientation is needed and what level of software would be appropriate to recommend. Sorting out the "real" question or the "real" desire can be difficult since the patron is often confused as to just what it is that a computer will do. Many simply do not understand the concept or need for a computer program.

A number of specific questions should be asked to determine essential facts, including: Have you been here before? Have you used an Apple (or whatever the library's brand of micro is) before? What software would you like? Simple questions such as these will give you rapid insight into whether the patron is familiar with the computer center services, rules and regulations, and whether he or she is a complete neophyte or is computer literate and has come to the library's center for a specific purpose. (Incidentally, it is important to ask if the patron has had experience with the particular brand of micro used in your library, rather than just asking "Have you used a micro before," since machines work differently.) It will become possible to determine—within seconds, 95% of the time—just how advanced a new patron is and how much help is required. The professional skill of most reference librarians will usually enable them to recommend software programs quickly and efficiently.

Scheduling

Libraries are advised to have patrons make appointments to use the computer and to stress this in all promotion about the service. Without scheduling, the public access program can quickly become chaotic.

Scheduling appointments should not take much time. If the publicity about the program has been effective, many people call for an appointment. Whether the appointment is made in person or over the telephone, the following rules will make life simpler.

1. Schedule appointments for one-hour periods. If this proves inappropriate, the time period can always be changed later. Patrons generally need and appreciate a full hour.

2. Allow no one to use more than three diskettes during any one appointment.

3. Allowing up to three people in the computer area at once is fine as long as one person has the appointment and the responsibility; the others are "guests." This type of arrangement is especially useful when dealing with children, who seem to learn better by interacting with one another. Adults often like to "bunch up" as well—it seems to make working with the computer less intimidating and more fun.

4. Don't allow people to make more than one appointment at a time. Some will ask to make a "regular" date each week ("I want to come in *every* Monday.") Assuming that the library has limited resources, patrons must wait their turn. Of course, if the library has acquired an over abundance of equipment, it may be possible to offer people a regular arrangement.

5. Use a substantial, durable book with a page for each day and adequate hourly notations to record appointments. Consider marking the names of first-time users with an asterisk, so that the librarian on duty will know what to expect when that patron arrives. If there seems to be a rash of missed appointments you may have to lay down some rules, such as, "If you miss two appointments you cannot reserve computer time for two weeks."

6. If patrons make the appointment in person, give them a slip with all essential information on it: library address, phone number, date and time of the appointment and so on (see Figure 4.1). Otherwise, 20% may forget to show up. Make children write down their appointments and, except in special circumstances, refuse to continue looking up appointments if they don't remember. They begin to remember very quickly.

7. It is advisable to have all computer patrons sign some form of user agreement. This should state clearly all the rules and regulations pertaining to use of the public access micro (see Figure 4.2).

8. It is a good idea to hold some form of identification when the patron checks out software to use with the computer. If you plan to do so, consider taking a driver's license or something similar. Many librarians have found that if they take library cards, at the end of the day a stack of cards is left behind.

Backup Assistance: When to Draw the Line

Regardless of their level of skill or computer expertise, most computer patrons will ask for assistance at some point. These requests usually fall into three categories: reference,

Managing the Project 61

Figure 4.1: North-Pulaski Computer Center Appointment Slip

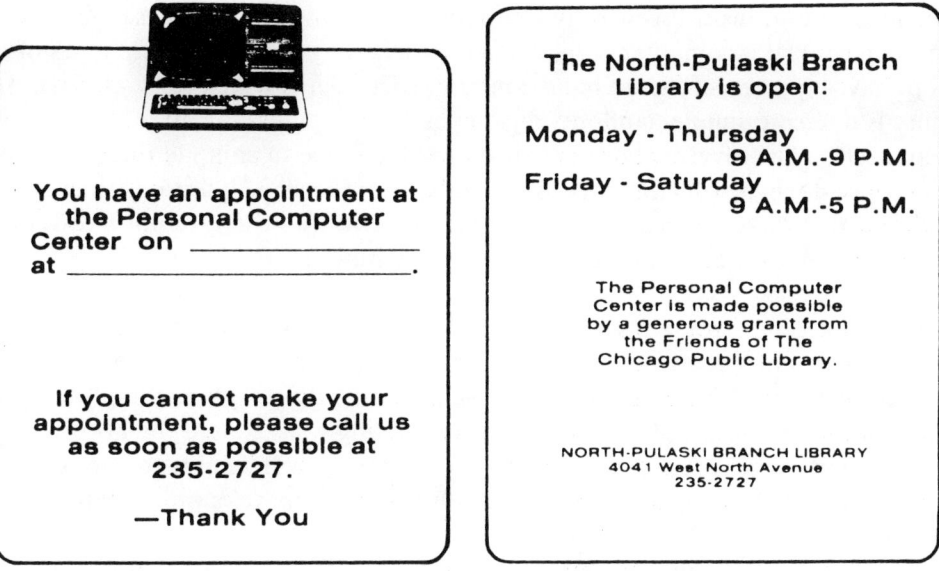

Front   Back

Figure 4.2: North-Pulaski User Agreement

THE CHICAGO PUBLIC LIBRARY, NORTH-PULASKI BRANCH,
THE PERSONAL COMPUTER CENTER, 4041 W. NORTH AVE., 235-2727,
PATRICK R. DEWEY, LIBRARIAN

USER AGREEMENT

1. The Personal Computer Center user agrees to take proper care of all equipment, diskettes, manuals, magazines, books, and all other equipment which is the property of The Chicago Public Library Personal Computer Center. When there is a fault with any equipment or materials, the user will immediately report any difficulty or problem to the System Operator (or available library employee).

2. User agrees to pay replacement cost of any equipment or materials lost or damaged as a result of carelessness by the user or failure to inform library employees of malfunctions.

3. User agrees to observe all copyright laws. User agrees not to duplicate any computer program or documentation provided by the library which is not in the public domain.

4. The Chicago Public Library makes no guarantees, either express or implied, with respect to any equipment, programs, or other library materials, their quality, performance, or fitness for any particular purpose. All materials and equipment are of a "demonstration" nature, and are given for use "as is". The ENTIRE risk as to the quality and performance of computer equipment/programs/documentation is with the user. In no event shall The Chicago Public Library be liable for actual, incidental or consequential damages in connection with or arising from the use of any equipment, programs, or other library materials.

5. Use of the equipment by patrons either per week or per month is not guaranteed. Time allotted is based as fairly as possible according to the demand placed upon the equipment by library patrons. From time to time, such events as "game days," seminars, classes, lectures or the like shall take precedence over normal computer use. All decisions as to the use of the computer and other library materials are at sole discretion of the Branch Manager or System Operator.

6. All users will supply their own recording media (diskettes, cassettes, etc.) when needed and any data lost as a result of faulty media, programs, etc. upon data storage is not the responsibility of The Chicago Public Library, its operators or employees. No private files may be stored at the library or on library media.

7. Failure to observe any part of the above agreement may result in a suspension of the user's right to use the Personal Computer Center. Other usual and ordinary library sanctions may also apply.

Signature   Date

"Help me, I'm stuck!" and questions that make the librarian want to scream.

Reference questions will generally be about how or where to purchase micros or software, how to contact a computer club, and so on. One way to handle these types of questions is to have a pamphlet file on hand containing frequently asked for materials. Another possibility is to create simple handouts of sources for computer education, lists of computer clubs, etc. The only drawback is that it does take time to compile these resources. However, once done, it will eliminate having to answer the same questions time and again. Make it clear that these materials are a ready reference only—they are not meant to endorse a particular brand of micro, software or institution.

Getting stuck in a program seems to afflict everyone sooner or later. Generally, the patron has accidentally gotten out of the program by hitting "reset" or some other key, as is evidenced by the flashing cursor on the screen. Getting the program going again is the only thing of importance, so don't waste time explaining what caused the problem. Just fix it, and then leave the area. After one or two visits, patrons will be able to correct such errors on their own. Helping a patron who is stuck should not take more than 30 seconds.

Questions in the last category range from amusing (Won't I get a better computer if I wait until the end of the year, or decade? Can it open my drapes?) to annoying (Can you set up my mailing list?). Most of these questions will come from adults; children seem to be more receptive to learning through experience at the microcomputer. Most questions pertaining to micro capabilities, or arising out of misconceptions about micros, are best dealt with by referring patrons to appropriate reading materials and, most important, by stressing that they will understand micros best by working with them.

Requests for assistance in setting up a data base, creating mailing lists, doing taxes, etc., will crop up when patrons use the sophisticated spreadsheet, word processing and DBMS programs. This may be one instance in which it is necessary to simply inform patrons that the staff is unable to assist with more than putting in the diskette. Patrons must understand that while librarians attempt to know something about the entire collection, some things require regular use to acquire proficiency.

CHARGING FOR SERVICES

Whether or not to charge for services is a decision that each library will face, and each must make this decision based on its own circumstances. My own feeling is that charging any more than a modest amount discourages use of the computer center by the disadvantaged and by children—the two groups most likely to need access to a public micro.

A number of libraries have found that a nominal charge, such as $1 per visit, is entirely acceptable to patrons and helps pay for and maintain the program (see Chapter 5). Others deal with coinop companies (discussed in Chapter 2) in order to charge patrons by the hour or per use. Many libraries simply collect money at the front desk or reference desk each time a patron uses the computer.

If you do decide to charge for services, do not charge more than the traffic will bear. Some libraries have started with a four- or five-dollar-an-hour fee only to lower it a few months later. It is also a good idea to give first-time patrons an hour free as a get-acquainted period.

The thorniest area of charging for services is how and whether to pass along the costs of online services. The debate over "fee or free" has raged since the introduction of these services in libraries, and public access micros will fuel it further. This issue is examined in Chapter 7.

MANAGING VOLUNTEERS

Most libraries are grateful for volunteers. If in recent years libraries have witnessed a decline in the spirit of voluntarism, perhaps the microcomputer will be responsible for a resurgence. Public access projects seem to attract volunteers from all segments of the community—from local computer clubs, universities, high schools, computer laboratories and among patrons who are computer enthusiasts. As the service is more widely advertised, people are bound to show up who will enjoy helping.

Such part-time helpers are particularly good at assisting and training other patrons and staff, but they may also assist with the bulletin board (electronic or paper) BASIC or other computer language classes and publicity. If someone talented comes along and there is a staff position suitable (such as a library page), you might consider hiring this person to help out exclusively with the micro operation. Generally, this will be someone who is still in school and needs part-time employment.

Be careful, however, that volunteers aren't volunteer "pirates." That is, their sole purpose cannot be to occupy the computer to duplicate (legally or otherwise) software, or to play arcade games because they ran out of quarters. Don't let them reserve all of the time for their friends. The most important caveat is to maintain control. Don't allow the volunteers to take over the whole operation. They may have some technical advice or skill, but they must work within the organizational structure.

SPECIAL CONSIDERATIONS FOR LENDING HARDWARE AND SOFTWARE

Advertising micros for loan will attract a great deal of interest. Even brief loan periods of one to two weeks will result in lengthy reserve lists. A few ways to keep hardware loan programs manageable include imposing a deposit until the micro is returned, setting up a "hot-line" for patrons to call when they have trouble with the equipment and establishing suitable overdue fines of, say, $1, $5 or more per day.

A carrying case should be provided to help protect the equipment and to keep it together with any software that is lent. (See the Downers Grove Public Library and Portsmouth Public Library sections in Chapter 5.)

Circulating software is not impossible; it just is not easy. If the library decides to lend software, it must consider the factors discussed below. One thing that must be kept in mind is that *only* public domain software can be considered for a software circulation program.

First, the library should never circulate its original programs, only copies. One library that circulated original diskettes found that it had to abandon its program. The Grace A. Dow Memorial Library (Midland, MI) had to discontinue its circulation of Apple disks, saying they have proved "too fragile a medium to withstand the rigors of circulation and exposure to disk drives with a variety of disk speeds." The library will continue to maintain its non-circulating public domain collection, which may be copied by computer patrons.[4]

The next, and perhaps most important consideration, is to protect the fragile diskettes. Provide each disk with its own permanent, plastic "library box." These cost about $2 or less when purchased in large quantities. Most patrons take care of the diskettes and losses at the few test sites around the country seem to be minimal.

A software circulation program has many benefits. It does bring new people into the library and is another way to help the library use the equipment more fully. It is also certain to generate a great amount of interest in the library's personal computer program. For example, a discussion of the North-Pulaski Branch Library public domain software collection in the December 1983 issue of *Popular Computing* generated hundreds of inquiries, including a number from churches, schools and clubs.

At the North Central Regional Library (Wenatchee, WA), the software circulation program has received an overwhelming response. According to Dean Marney, computer services coordinator, the program was introduced at a local computer fair. More than 500 pieces of software were checked out in little over half a day. The operation calls for a master set of the public domain material plus many blank diskettes. When a patron asks for a specific disk from the catalog, a fresh one is produced on the spot. This solves the problem of running out of an advertised item. Sturdy boxes are used to circulate the material. (See also the Alice and Hamilton Fish Library discussion in Chapter 5.)

A WORD ABOUT COMPUTER ABUSE

" 'War Game' Is Up For Nuclear Computer Raiders" and other headlines have recently been in the news. They are primarily reports about youthful computer buffs who have managed to break into various computer networks. Even though it is unlikely that the library's microcomputer will be used for such an illegal activity, librarians must be alert to the possibility. By exercising good judgment and monitoring the computer center regularly, librarians can discourage such activities.

Piracy is another example of improper use of the library's public computer. People who flagrantly violate the copyright laws by copying proprietary software make it more expensive for the rest of us. Software piracy takes place wherever there are people who want to trade software, and the library is not immune. Do not allow the library to become a meeting ground for software pirates. It is always possible that a library can get into serious trouble as a result of any illegal copying activity that takes place on its premises. At the very least, post a sign forbidding copying of commercial programs. It is also advisable to have patrons sign a statement that spells out the copyright law and absolves the library of any liability.

FEEDBACK: EVALUATING THE PROJECT

From time to time, the library should evaluate its public access effort to determine whether improvements are needed or if the community's needs have changed.

A simple form to collect data is essential to keep track of how many programs are being used. It should not take patrons more than a minute or so to fill out. It is not necessary to have every patron fill out a form every day. A random sampling taken 12 or even two times a year will be sufficient.

Be interested enough in the project to talk with patrons about the programs and services offered. Many will have a great awareness of the latest advances in popular software, and their opinions can be valuable.

As the project matures, you may find that changes will be made regarding staff responsibilities or various library policies. Also, as pointed out earlier, patrons' needs and expectations will broaden as their skills develop, and additional services and library activities will be required to meet the demand.

NOTES

1. See "Buyer's Guide to Computer Furniture" in the September 1983 issue of *Personal Computing*.

2. Leslie Edmonds, "Taming Technology: Planning for Patron use of Microcomputers in the Public Library," *Top of the News* 39 (Spring 1983): 250.

3. Linda Ward Callaghan, "Children's Questions: Reference Interviews with the Young," in *The Reference Librarian*, edited by William K. Katz and Ruth A. Fraley (New York: Hayworth Press, 1983), p. 55.

4. *Library Hotline* (December 19, 1983): 5

5

Examples of Public Access Projects

There are many libraries doing exciting things with public access microcomputers. It is obviously quite impossible to document them all here. The projects discussed in this chapter are noteworthy because of special applications, problems that required solution or, in some cases, the equipment that was used. The information given in each reflects these criteria. Details about the projects are summarized in Table 5.1.

ALICE AND HAMILTON FISH LIBRARY
Box 265
Garrison, NY 10524
Contact: Geraldine Mahoney (914) 424-3020

Alice and Hamilton Fish is one of the few libraries to circulate software. According to Ms. Mahoney, library director, 894 diskettes circulated in a six-month period ending in June 1983. The public access project began in early 1982 with a $2000 grant from the Mid-Hudson Library System. Initially, the library planned to buy software for a variety of machines. Ultimately, the decision was made to stay with software for one micro, the Apple.

Diskettes are stored and lent in durable, plastic library boxes. All software is purchased from Ted Sherman, a vendor in New York. The vendor replaces any diskettes that have worn out. The library makes backup copies of all important programs before allowing them to circulate.

Although the library feared that losses might be significant, the loss rate turned out to be very low. When compared to holdings, software is the highest circulating item in the library.

Table 5.1: Comparison of Library Public Access Projects

Name	Service Population	Equipment*	Fees Charged	Service	Funding/Source
Alice and Hamilton Fish Library (rural)	6,500	Apple II	Free	On-site use, lend software	$2000 grant (software only)
Chicago Public Library†					
North-Pulaski Branch (urban)	82,393	Apple II, modem, printer	Free	On-site use, public domain copying, electronic BBS, wall charts, electronic delivery of software	$4370 (Friends of the Library)
Douglass Branch (urban)	60,534	Commodore 64	Free	On-site use	$500 (patron gift), $3600 (Illinois Humane Society)
Rockwell Gardens Reading and Study Center (low-income housing project)	7,000	Commodore PET 2001 (5), Commodore PET 4032	Free	On-site use	Anonymous donor
Sherman Park Branch (urban)	59,075	Apple II	Free	On-site use	$3000 (LSCA funds)
ComputerTown USA!					
Menlo Park Public Library (suburban)	26,150	Apple IIe, Atari 400, Commodore PET (4), TRS-80	Free	On-site use	Grant (National Science Foundation)
Upper Arlington Public Library (suburban)	833,250	Apple IIe, Atari 400, Commodore 64, Hewlett-Packard, IBM PC, Osborne, VIC 20 (several)	Free	On-site use, lend hardware (VIC 20)	Gifts from computer companies, CompuServe, Warner-Amex Qube
Downers Grove Public Library (suburban)	42,691	Timex-Sinclair (7)	Free	Lend hardware	Friends of the Library
Frankfort Public Library (suburban)	12,353	Apple II	$2 per hour	On-site use	Originally purchased as backup to circulation system

Table 5.1: Comparison of Library Public Access Projects (cont.)

Name	Service Population	Equipment*	Fees Charged	Service	Funding/Source
Liverpool Public Library (suburban)	50,049	Apple II+ (2), printer, disk drives	Free	On-site use	$2000 (state aid), $2000 (revenue-sharing), $900 (Friends of the Library), $800 (Rotary Club)
Maywood Public Library (suburban)	27,998	Apple II, Apple IIe, printer (2), Amdek color monitor (2), disk drives	Free	On-site use	State per capita grant
Portsmouth Public Library (suburban)	26,000	Apple II, Commodore VIC 20 (4)	Free, $10 rental	On-site use, lend hardware	Gifts from local store, purchased by library trustees
Rolling Meadows Library (suburban)	20,167	Apple II, disk drives	Free	On-site use	$3000 (revenue-sharing), $300 (Friends of the Library), library budget
Scottsdale Public Library (suburban)	100,000	Apple IIe, TI 99/4A (2), monitor (2), disk drives	Free	On-site use	Gifts from Texas Instruments, library Trust Account
Southern Adirondack Library System (rural)	100,000	Apple II+ (11), disk drives, Hayes Micromodem (11), Sanyo monitors (11)	Free	On-site use, adult computer literacy program	$41,000 (LSCA Title I grant), Special Purpose Grant, other grants
Wilmette Public Library (suburban)	28,229	Apple II, Epson MX-70 printer	$2 per hour	On-site use	Bequest, community groups, Friends of the Library

*Numbers in parentheses ( ) indicate multiple units.
† Several other CPL branch libraries also have public access equipment. The ones listed here were selected because of special equipment configuration, application, location or funding.

CALIFORNIA STATE LIBRARY
914 Capitol Mall
Library and Courts Building
PO Box 2037
Sacramento, CA 95809
Contact: Liz Gibson (916) 323-5491

In January 1984 the California State Library, in conjunction with the People's Computer Co. (see the ComputerTown USA! discussion below), received a $500,000 Library Services and Construction Act (LSCA) Title I grant for a statewide computer literacy project. The project will provide computer literacy training sessions to staff members from 85 California public libraries that have, or are in the process of installing, public access micros. In return, the libraries will be expected to set up computer literacy programs for their adult service populations. Each library will receive $1000 to help defray administrative costs. Funding for equipment purchases is the responsibility of each participating library.

Twelve of these libraries will be established as regional resource centers, to train any new staff members and assist the staff and patrons of the remaining 73 libraries when the training periods are over. These resource centers will be awarded $20,000 each for hardware and software purchases. The California State Library and the People's Computer Co. suggest that the resource center libraries use $15,000 to purchase four to five micros and the remaining $5000 to purchase software. No additional funding will be allotted for library staff time as the agreement stipulates that the resource centers must bear that cost.

CHICAGO PUBLIC LIBRARY
425 N. Michigan Ave.
Chicago, IL 60611
(312) 269-2900
Contact: Patrick R. Dewey (312) 235-2727

A number of public access experiments and projects have taken place in the Chicago Public Library (CPL) system. Most of the early projects were ushered in during the period that Donald Sager was commissioner of libraries (1978-1981). Sager must be credited with foresight and innovation for the implementation of public access.

Initially, Speak N' Spell microchip units were introduced at all CPL branch libraries, and were an immediate hit with children. These simple units were used for spelling practice and had add-on math modules as well. The problems encountered with this program were high noise level (the units were used in the library, not circulated) and theft. The only staff involvement consisted of dispensing the units and replacing batteries. The micros were eventually equipped with AC adapters instead of batteries, headsets to eliminate noise and chains to prevent theft.

In 1979 the first true microcomputers were introduced. Six Commodore PET 2001s were installed: two in each of two branch libraries, and one unit in each of two other branches.[1] Although these micros had only 8K of memory, they were selected because of their compactness and low cost. Each micro came with a built-in tape drive and monitor, for a cost of $600 per unit. Approximately $1000 was budgeted for yearly software acquisitions (tapes, magazines and books) at each location.

Unfortunately, the machines were deficient in other areas. The keyboard was substandard, which made typing difficult, and the tape drives were inaccurate and slow. Since the machines had to be sent out for maintenance (it could not be performed locally), service delays were lengthy, sometimes taking as long as eight months. The theft of two units further aggravated the problems.

On the whole, the PET experience was still considered successful. Despite numerous problems, the machines were extremely popular and provided a clear, objective look at the difficulties that would be encountered with a public access service. It was with these lessons in mind that new public access projects were initiated at North-Pulaski and, later, at several other CPL branch libraries. (The grant proposal for the North-Pulaski project is reproduced in Appendix A.)

North-Pulaski Branch Library
4041 W. North Ave.
Chicago, IL 60639
Contact: Patrick Dewey (312) 235-2727

The Personal Computer Center at North-Pulaski began operation in November 1981. An Apple II+ computer was selected for several reasons: staff familiarity (the author, a staff member, owned an Apple for several years), the Apple's good reputation and marketing appeal, its reliability and the large quantity of software available for it.

The equipment configuration is 64K RAM (which replaced the original 48K integer firmware card), two disk drives, a printer and a modem. This makes it possible to use most of the programs available for the Apple computer. Enhancements such as a CP/M-card and an 80-column card were not added because of financial considerations. The budget clearly restricted the level of service.

Software has been obtained free from a number of sources, including clubs, patron gifts and donations from companies, as well as being purchased. As of this writing, North-Pulaski Library owns more than 1000 programs on more than 175 diskettes.

The machine is housed in a small room of its own to afford better security and to allow patrons a degree of privacy. Also, this eliminates the problem of crowds forming around the machine, which had occurred with the PETs. It was decided to give each patron a minimum of assistance, including a brief, five-minute orientation and followup assistance to help with minor problems. The public access program is designed to appeal to patrons of all ages, and is marketed to adults and children alike. Service is not divided into juvenile and adult periods.

Initially, arcade games were allowed at any time, but this became unmanageable. "Arcade Game Days" were instituted, but the response was so overwhelming that this

A young patron uses the Apple computer at the North-Pulaski Personal Computer Center.

activity, too, was discontinued. Arcade games are no longer allowed in the personal computer center. Many other types of games are included in the software collection, and the library has an arrangement for free time on Gamemaster, a local computer game network (see Chapter 6).

The usage pattern during the first year was very good. Adults comprised approximately 40% of all users. As of 1984 anywhere from 200 to 400 people use the machine in any given month. All age groups use the micro in equal amounts, except for senior citizens and preschoolers, who use it less than 1% each.

With the aid of volunteer instructors, the Personal Computer Center at North-Pulaski has also offered microcomputer-based courses in BASIC and ASSEMBLY programming languages. The BASIC class attracted 160 applicants in just one week. (Only 40 people could enroll.) A two-hour "Word Processing Seminar" given by a local businessperson attracted approximately 40 people on a Saturday morning. The staff plans to repeat this seminar each year. Roger Sutton, children's librarian at North-Pulaski, has been using the Apple computer to supplement story hour with various age groups, including preschoolers.

North-Pulaski also operates a bulletin board system that patrons can call from home. Patrons can read and leave messages, and access a number of feature articles. Most recently, the library has begun to provide electronic delivery of software to patrons via the system. The bulletin board system is discussed in Chapter 7.

Douglass Branch Library
3353 W. 13th St.
Chicago, IL 60608
Contact: Eloise Little (312) 762-3725

The Douglass Branch Library began its public access program in mid-1983, when it received a Commodore 64 micro, color monitor and one disk drive free as a demonstration model from the vendor. The library purchased 629 educational software programs out of regular library materials funds.

The library planned a number of activities, including "Computer Tutor," a tutoring project for students. Older children are recruited to teach younger students at the computer center. As of July 1983 60 people per day were using the facility.

In late 1983 the library received a $3600 grant for the program from the Illinois Humane Society. It plans to use the money to purchase the demonstration equipment, along with a second disk drive and a printer, and to add an Apple IIe with dual disk drives. Additional software will also be purchased.

Rockwell Gardens Reading and Study Center
2515 W. Jackson Blvd.
Chicago, IL 60612
Contact: Marie Baker (312) 243-4534

The Rockwell Gardens Reading and Study Center houses five Commodore PET 2001 micros, received from an anonymous donor. Its public access program is geared to giving remedial help to students in math and reading. A master instruction system (consisting of a PET 4032 micro with dual drives and a printer) is used to maintain student scores and records.

The project, called the Homework Resource Center, began in September 1983. One hundred and twenty young people registered for the program, including 60 elementary and 60 high school students. Students are given a pretest, a curriculum of books and learning materials to follow, a post-test and a new curriculum. Each student is given four hours per week to use the equipment. Ms. Baker reports that "the microcomputer has rekindled an interest in learning."

Sherman Park Branch Library
5440 S. Racine Ave.
Chicago, IL 60609
Contact: Emily Guss (312) 268-4377

The Sherman Park public access project began in mid-1983 with a $3000 grant from LSCA Title III Grants for Community Interlibrary Cooperative Projects. Funds were used to purchase an Apple II micro with one disk drive, a printer and a modem. The library provides a year-round tutoring program at its computer center for students from the nearby Arthur Libby Elementary School. Students are assisted with basic skills such as reading and spelling.

COMPUTERTOWN USA!
People's Computer Co.
PO Box E
Menlo Park, CA 94025
Contact: Nancy Mullenaux (415) 323-3111

ComputerTown USA! is a computer literacy project of the People's Computer Co., a nonprofit organization in Menlo Park (CA). It offers its services to any library, educational institution or business that wishes to establish a public access computer literacy project. Its goals include giving "everyone in the community an opportunity to become 'computer literate' in an informal educational setting."

There has not been much coordination between affiliates, but ComputerTown is trying to improve this. A 100-page Implementation Package is now offered containing sample forms, outlines of "playdays," "business nights" and other suggestions for activities. Membership fees range from $15 to $100 and include the following categories: personal, leader, group and commercial.

People's Computer Co. publishes *ComputerTown News Bulletin*, which is a good source of information for program ideas and problem-solving strategies. Guidebooks are also available, including *Microcomputer Questions and Answers, A Bay Area Guide to Computer Stores* and *A Buyer's Guide to the Right Computer*. Two ComputerTown projects are described below.

Menlo Park Public Library
Laurel and Alma Sts.
Menlo Park, CA 94025
Contact: Doreen Cohen (415) 858-3462

The Menlo Park Public Library was the original test site for the ComputerTown USA! project. The project, called ComputerTown Menlo Park, began in 1979 and was seen as "a place where people of all ages have access to computers." Four micros located in the reading room of the library gave many people in the community the chance to enjoy a variety of activities. These included workshops, "business nights," volunteer tutoring programs and transportation of the computers to other locations in the community. Many of the basic rules now suggested in the Implementation Package, were, in fact, worked out at this site.[2] In 1981 a grant to further the project was received from the National Science Foundation. Funds from this grant were used to purchase an Apple IIe micro. The library also received three used micros—a Commodore PET, an Atari 400 and a TRS-80—as gifts. In early 1984, Menlo Park was selected as a regional resource center for the California State Library's new computer literacy project, discussed earlier.

Upper Arlington Public Library
2800 Tremont Rd.
Upper Arlington, OH 43221
Contact: Russell E. Walker (614) 486-9621

ComputerTown Upper Arlington is the "eastern model ComputerTown." the following equipment has been donated to the library for public use: a Commodore 64 (from

CompuServe), an Apple IIe, Texas Instruments 99/4A and an Osborne (from local computer stores), an Atari 400 (from Warner-Amex Qube) and a Hewlett-Packard (from Hewlett-Packard). The library expects to receive an IBM PC from a local computer store in March 1984. The library also lends Commodore VIC 20s to patrons. The library thus has samples of most major types of microcomputers for patrons to try out.

The library offers computer classes three times a week, both morning and evening. It relies heavily on volunteers to train patrons.

DOWNERS GROVE PUBLIC LIBRARY
1050 Curtiss Street
Downers Grove, IL 60515
Contact: Kathryn Balcolm (312) 960-1200

The Downers Grove Public Library is one of the few libraries able to circulate microcomputers. The library experienced a tremendous response when five Timex-Sinclair machines were made available for patrons to take home: six months of reserves were taken in less than two weeks. The library's central goal, as stated in the original grant proposal to the Friends of the Library, is "to increase general computer literacy among patrons and to allow individuals to assess their interest in computers before personally investing in equipment." The program was originally funded as a six-month pilot project. However, it was so successful that funding was extended.

Ownership, repair and replacement of equipment rest with the Friends of the Library. All patrons must have a valid adult library card from the library. Anyone under 14 years of age must have the consent of a parent or guardian.

The materials provided include the micro, power supply, a TV adapter, instruction booklet and carrying case. No software is supplied. The staff will assist patrons with set-up problems but not with programming techniques. A list of volunteers who will help patrons at home over the phone is also available. The loan period is seven days and is not renewable. Overdue fines are $1 per day.

The project had a kick-off event in December 1982, featuring a demonstration of the machine's capabilities. Names were drawn from a hat to select the first patrons to get the machines. The press release publicizing this event is reprinted in Figure 5.1.

An evaluation of the program in April 1983 revealed "no major problems, no losses and no damage." Fifty of 64 patrons responding to a survey expressed the belief that the library should support such a service financially. Many also indicated that they would like software to go along with the machine. Almost no overdue fines have been collected, since most equipment is returned on time. Because of the success of the project, several additional micros have been added.

Figure 5.1: Downers Grove Public Access Press Release

> Library patrons in Downers Grove will soon have the chance to introduce themselves to the ever-growing world of computers.
>
> In an experimental program sponsored by the Downers Grove Friends of the Library, Timex/Sinclair computers will be lent to Downers Grove Public Library adult-card holders.
>
> The library patrons who borrow these small-but-powerful computers for one-week acquaintance loans will use their own TV set for displaying computer output. If it is desired to save programs that are developed, audio cassette recorders can be used.
>
> Computers on loan will be accompanied by a TV adapter and cable, a power supply for the computer, connecting cables for the cassette recorder, and an instruction manual.
>
> The first computers will be lent to patrons at the end of a kick-off party at the library at 2:00 p.m. on December 12. At this event the computers will be demonstrated and the attendees will have a chance to try them out. The afternoon will be concluded with a drawing of names to determine which patrons will check out the five computers on December 12, and the order of the rest of the patrons' names on the reserve list.
>
> Further information will be available in the Downers Grove Public Library where one of the computers will present a message (stored in computer memory) on a TV monitor that will describe the lending program and the kick-off event.

Reprinted courtesy Downers Grove Public Library.

FRANKFORT PUBLIC LIBRARY
Route 30 and Pfeiffer Rd.
Frankfort, IL 60423
Contact: Arlene Santoro (815) 469-2423

The Frankfort Public Library began its public access project in 1980. It has the longest running program in Illinois. The original Apple micro was purchased partly with grant money and partly with library capital expenditures funds. It was intended mainly as a backup for the library's automated circulation system, and patrons were allowed to use it only on an occasional basis at a charge of $1 per half hour. However, public demand soon grew. A second micro—purchased with the monies collected from users—has been added, exclusively for public access. The fees collected can amount to $200 per month, and allow for the purchase of additional software, paper, ribbons and diskettes.

Occasional workshops on computer literacy are given by staff members and last for about one hour followed by question-and-answer periods. The workshops were originally offered for adults and junior high levels, but the juvenile sections were discontinued when it was discovered that area schools with computers were providing the same service to students.

As of this writing, the library owns about 70 diskettes of programs. New software is purchased monthly. The purchase of Wizardry, a high resolution graphics "Dungeons and Dragons" game, immediately produced a group of enthusiastic followers. The library has since acquired a good collection of such games, ranging from simple to complex, in addition to educational and other types of programs.

All patrons must reserve time to use the computer, and follow the guidelines for computer use. The Frankfort guidelines for microcomputer use are reprinted in Figure 5.2. Ms. Santoro feels that the good public relations resulting from the project has been a very positive contribution to the library.

Figure 5.2: Frankfort Public Library Microcomputer Guidelines

---

The Board Of Trustees of the
Frankfort Public Library District
is experimenting with public access
to the 48K Apple II microcomputer.

GUIDELINES FOR USE OF THE APPLE COMPUTER

1. Use is by reservation only.

2. Preschool children must be accompanied by an adult until such time as the child's competency has been ascertained.

3. Since we do not have staff trained to teach computer literacy to individuals, access is limited to those who have learned how to operate this specific microcomputer, either through classroom or independent study. Time will have to be forfeited if the user is not sufficiently self directed.

4. The unit is not fragile. The user, however, is liable for any damage caused by misuse or mistreatment.

5. There will be no charge for use related to library programs, or for cooperative programs with other local government agencies. Fees for other use will be determined by the Board of Trustees.

Reprinted courtesy of the Frankfort Public Library.

LIVERPOOL PUBLIC LIBRARY
Tulip and Second Sts.
Liverpool, NY 13088
Contact: Jean Armour (315) 457-0310

Faye Golden, director of the Liverpool Public Library, and Jean Armour, assistant director for public services, have been the moving force behind development of two computer facilities for library patrons. The first is a private study area called Pascal Place, which houses an Apple II+ micro. The computer is equipped with 64K and a PASCAL language system as well as Applesoft BASIC. The Pascal Place Apple also has a 132-

78   PUBLIC ACCESS MICROCOMPUTERS

Pascal Place is one of two friendly and well-organized computer centers at the Liverpool Public Library.

column Epson MX-80 printer, lower case adapter, two disk drives and an 80-column green screen. The equipment is suitable for word processing, data base management and other business applications. No games are permitted in Pascal Place. In a different location, the library has a second Apple II+ computer intended for general public access. The micro has 48K RAM and color capability. Games are allowed at this location.

Ms. Armour and two assistants oversee the public access operation, which is free. All patrons must complete a general orientation session in order to use the equipment. At these sessions, patrons are given a description of the microcomputers and software available. Extensive patron worksheets have been worked out for patron training.

Attractive promotional material and active staff participation have led to public acceptance and appreciation of the project. The library also sponsors a number of computer-related activities. One special event that has been very successful is "Data Factory Night." This gives participants a general introduction to data base management programs. An excellent five-page flyer, "Making Data Factory Work For You," has been prepared to assist patrons with these programs.

Other materials prepared by the library include "How to Copy Your Disk" and various "help" sheets for high resolution graphics games such as Cranston Manor and Ulysses and the Golden Fleece.

The library plans to expand the project as budgetary considerations and time allow. The library also foresees circulating software in the future.

MAYWOOD PUBLIC LIBRARY
121 S. Fifth Ave.
Maywood, IL 60153
Contact: Stan Huntington (312) 343-1847

The Maywood public access project began in February 1983. Since the project's inception, the library has acquired approximately 50 program diskettes to go with its Apple II micro. The computer has 64K RAM, dual disk drive and is equipped with an Amdek color monitor. The library also makes an Okidata 82A printer available to the public. A second micro, an Apple IIe, an Apple printer and Amdek color monitor were purchased in January 1984. The library has a service contract with a local vendor, which it obtains at a reduced rate. The machine is serviced locally on a carry-in basis.

The equipment is housed in a special room along with the library's fiche reader, video tape player and other audiovisual hardware. A high school student was hired as a "computer assistant" to help patrons and to maintain the software library, which includes programs such as Screenwriter II, VisiCalc and Apple LOGO.

All patrons must attend a group orientation session before using the computer. Orientation is given in small groups twice a week or on an individual basis, and includes the demonstration of several programs. Before using any of the equipment, patrons must sign a "User's Agreement." Librarians at the information desk schedule patrons for time at the computer. The service is free.

PORTSMOUTH PUBLIC LIBRARY
8 Islington St.
Portsmouth, NH 03801
Contact: Sue McCann (603) 431-2000

The Portsmouth Public Library has an Apple II computer for use by patrons in the library and four Commodore VIC 20s, which it makes available for patrons to take home. Two of the VIC 20s were purchased by the library trustees and two were donated by a local computer store. The loan periods for the VIC 20s are 12 days, maximum. The periods are scheduled so that at least one machine is available for the Saturday computer clinic held each week at the library. To borrow a machine, patrons must show three forms of valid identification, be at least 21 years of age and be a borrower in good standing.

The computer loan package includes all of the necessary hardware to connect the machine to the patron's home TV (e.g., switchbox, RF modulator), a Commodore joystick, power supply, manual and a carrying case to keep everything together. Also included are various user manuals, a cartridge, a business program on cassette and a list of the package contents.

Patrons must pay a $25 cash deposit to borrow the package. Ten dollars is the loan fee; the remainder is refunded if the machine is returned in working order. Late fines are $10 the first day and $5 for each additional day. As of mid-1983, only one person had returned the material late. No software or books have been lost. In the one instance where a machine broke down, it turned out to be cheaper to buy a replacement than to have it fixed.

Portsmouth has set up per-day time limits to govern use of the in-house Apple. They are computer games, one-half hour; chess, one hour; instructional use, one hour; personal programming, one hour; course work in connection with courses offered at the library, two hours. Staff members were trained both at the computer store from which the Apple was purchased and by a computer consultant hired by the library. Some staff members have received instruction on the VisiCalc and WordStar programs. The library is contemplating the purchase of additional equipment in the future.

ROLLING MEADOWS LIBRARY
3110 Martin Lane
Rolling Meadows, IL 60008
Contact: Cheryl A. Nordlund (312) 259-6050

Since the early 1970s, Rolling Meadows Library has had a computer terminal in place which ties into the mainframe computer of the local school district. Students use the terminal to do computer-related homework. Leslie Edmonds, children's librarian and the person responsible for public access computer development, realized that there were a number of problems with using this arrangement for public access, including the difficulty of staff training, scheduling and repair—it was actually necessary to send the terminal out of state for maintenance.

The library's adult and juvenile departments decided jointly that a microcomputer was needed to replace the terminal. The library received a $300 grant from the Friends of the Library and $3000 in federal revenue-sharing money from the township to purchase equipment. Software was purchased with funds from the library's audiovisual budget.

The library acquired a 48K, dual-drive Apple computer and placed it with the audiovisual collection. A separate location away from the flow would have been preferable, but this would not have afforded the same security as the audiovisual location. The present location also serves as a convenient depot for the checkout and return of diskettes.

Rolling Meadows has established clearly defined policies regarding hardware, software, scheduling and patron responsibility. Patrons must have a valid Rolling Meadows Library card in order to use the equipment, and the library runs weekly orientation workshops that can accommodate 10 to 12 patrons at a time. Younger users must have a parent or guardian sign a responsibility statement. Figures 5.3 and 5.4 reprint the rules and sample worksheets for the patron workshops. The service is free to patrons.

SCOTTSDALE PUBLIC LIBRARY
3839 Civic Center Plaza
Scottsdale, AZ 85251
Contact: Judy Register (602) 994-2471

The Scottsdale Public Library instituted its public access project in two phases. Phase One began when Texas Instruments donated two TI 99/4A micros to the library. Software and monitors were purchased with funds from the library's Trust Account.

The main users of this equipment are children from 3 to 13 years old. (Those under seven must come with an adult.) Computer time is scheduled in 30-minute blocks, and appointments must be made in advance either in person or by telephone. All users must attend a computer orientation program before using the equipment.

The equipment is kept in a 6-foot by 8-foot corner of the Children's Room in the library. It is available for use 51 hours per week. Software consists of TI Command Modules, for ages 3 and up. Subjects include spelling, reading, touch typing, math and a game, Hangman. Only library-owned software is used, since the equipment cannot accommodate other types of programs.

Phase Two of the project began in January 1983 when the library acquired an Apple IIe. This micro is housed in a different location and is intended for adult use. The software available for the Apple includes word processing, data base management and speed-reading programs.

Figure 5.3: Rolling Meadows Library Computer Rules

We hope you enjoy using the Apple II Computer. It is a service that the library is happy to offer. However, to insure that the service runs smoothly, we need your cooperation with the following rules.

1. If you wish to use the Apple, you must complete the Rolling Meadows Library Apple Workshop or demonstrate your ability to use an Apple by passing a use test. You must also sign a responsibility statement. Your Rolling Meadows Library card will be stamped with an identifying mark to show that you are a registered user.

2. To make an appointment to use the Apple, you may call or come in ON THE DAY you wish to use it. Substitutions cannot be made. If a cancellation occurs, the time becomes free for the next person who calls or comes in. If you cancel more than once in one day, you will not be allowed to use the Apple any time during the day.

3. When you come to use the Apple you must leave your library card at the circulation desk before you log on. NO substitute cards of any kind will be accepted (this includes family members and friends). Only Rolling Meadows Library cards will be accepted.

4. Software disks may be checked out from the circulation desk for in the library use only. If a disk is lost or damaged, the user will be charged the cost of replacement of the disk plus a $3 processing fee. Users are free to bring disks from home to use with our Apple.

5. Due to the demand to use the Apple, scheduling will be done in half-hour periods. If you are using the Apple and find that no one has been scheduled for the next time slot, you may continue until a new user who has not had an opportunity to use the Apple arrives and signs up to use it. Scheduled appointments will be held for 10 minutes for latecomers, then the time will be given to someone else.

6. Only two people can use the Apple at one time. We will give one warning and then the Apple will be shut down until the next appointment.

7. If the Apple is down during a particular time period, the regular schedule will continue and lost time will NOT be added on or made up.

8. Members of the library staff have the right to cancel or interrupt use of the Apple.

Abuse of the rules will result in discontinued use of service. Library staff has the right to restrict usage for those people who cannot abide by the regulations of the library as a whole or the specific regulations governing the use of the terminal.

Reprinted courtesy of the Rolling Meadows Library

Figure 5.4: Rolling Meadows Library Apple Computer Worksheet

(correct answers are supplied in parentheses following each exercise question.)

To Log On

1. Turn on the monitor.

2. Put disk in _____. (disk drive #1)

3. Turn on power switch—back, left corner of terminal.

4. Use _____ command if you need a list of what is on the disk. (catalog)

5. Follow directions on the disk. Check _____ next to Apple if you need help. (notebook)

6. To "boot" a disk, use _____ command. Whenever possible, use this instead of on/off switch. (PR#6)

7. If _____ on the disk drive is on, DO NOT: 1. Take disk out, 2. Hit the reset key or 3. Turn off power. (red light)

Useful Tips

1. What are the following for?

RETURN: (This is the enter key)

Cursor: (Square light on screen that indicates that you may type a command)

RESET: (Will bring you back to the beginning of the program)

ESC: (Stands for "escape," will get you out of a program)

CNTL: (Stands for "control" and is used as part of some commands)

To Log Off

1. Take the disk out of the disk drive and return it to _____. (circulation desk)

2. Pick up _____. (your library card)

Activities

1. Use two different disks.

2. Bring your library card with you and come to the workshop next week.

Reprinted courtesy of the Rolling Meadows Library

SOUTHERN ADIRONDACK LIBRARY SYSTEM
22 Whitney Place
Saratoga Springs, NY 12866
Contact: Marcene Rose (518) 584-7300

In fall 1982 the Southern Adirondack Library System received a New York State Library Services and Construction Act Title I grant of $41,000 to establish computer literacy programs in eight libraries in the system's primarily rural service area. Each library received an Apple II+ microcomputer with two disk drives, 64K RAM and 12-inch Sanyo green monitors. The project was expanded, through additional grants, to include four more libraries for a total service population of more than 100,000.

Like the California State Library project discussed earlier, Southern Adirondack's program is aimed at the adult population. Formal training sessions involving more than 100 volunteers and staff were begun at most locations. By the end of the grant period, 3000 adults had participated in the program, and most library staff members had become computer literate.

With the help of several area service organizations and Friends of the Library groups, the system is now planning a second phase of the project. In September 1983 Hayes Micromodems were purchased for all libraries with microcomputers. These will allow online access to consumer data bases and may eventually be used for system networking. Other plans include establishing electronic bulletin board systems and the purchase of additional equipment at some locations.

Ms. Marcene Rose, project coordinator, states that the "goal of increasing adult microcomputer literacy has been accomplished but even more important, the microcomputers have enhanced libraries' images as up-to-date resource centers."

WILMETTE PUBLIC LIBRARY
1442 Wilmette Ave.
Wilmette, IL 60091
Contact: Richard Thompson (312) 256-5035

The Wilmette Public Library has borrowed the storyline of a book, *The Phantom Toll Booth*, as the theme for its public access micro center. In the book, a young person builds a "phantom toll booth" where, upon inserting a coin, he can enter a fantasy world of numbers and words. In the same fashion, the Wilmette library has installed a coinbox next to its micro which is housed in a glass-walled area called the Phantom Toll Booth. Patrons purchase tokens at the circulation desk in order to operate the micro. The tokens cost 50 cents each and last for 15 minutes. (The library originally charged $1, but dropped the price to increase usage.) The monies collected will be used to help purchase additional computers and software.

Much of the remodeling and equipment was donated, including a bequest for one-third the cost of the room. Additional funds were provided by the Friends of the Library and another community organization.

Computer time is by appointment and can be scheduled up to one week in advance. A valid Wilmette library card is required along with a second form of identification, such as a school ID or driver's license.

The library produces a software list for patrons, with suggested age levels for each item. Some of the software available is: Checkers, Castle Wolfenstein, Scott Adams' Adventures, Ultima, Ernie's Quiz and Painter Power. Programming languages include: Applesoft BASIC, Apple LOGO, Apple PASCAL, Integer BASIC, Microsoft BASIC (M BASIC). *Perfect Writer*, a word processing program, is available to patrons. To save time, patrons can purchase pre-formatted blank disks at the circulation desk for $3 each. As of this writing, there is only one Apple II with an Epson MX-70 printer, but the library plans to buy two additional Apple computers, including an Apple IIe with peripherals. The room is large enough to accommodate the additional equipment.

NOTES

1. *Annual Report of the Microcomputer Committee* (Chicago, IL: The Chicago Public Library, 1980).

2. Doreen Cohen, "Public Access Micros," *Access* 2 (October 1982): 5.

6

Clubs, Special Events and Other Activities

Libraries can sponsor a number of computer-related activities for patrons. These can be ongoing programs, such as classes or clubs, or one-time events, such as contests or game days. As noted earlier, when planning any microcomputer-related event, it is important to take the needs of the library and the total community into account. Never run activities or programs at the expense of other important reference or library services. Strive for a healthy balance between computer services and books, and between activities and manpower.

The following are activities that have worked successfully at libraries. All have the public access micro as their central theme. Some—such as the Pac Man art contest or computer reading contest—will work just as well for libraries that do not have a public access micro. In this way, even a library that does not have or need a public access micro can capitalize on the popularity of micros and benefit from the interest they generate.

COMPUTER CLUBS

Computer clubs are one of the most successful types of ongoing activities a library can institute. They work well for all age groups and can be formed around a variety of interests. They often have the added advantage of attracting new patrons and potential volunteers to the library. A number of different approaches are described below.

Young Adult Computer Club

Young people like to congregate, and a regular computer club that meets weekly for an hour or so can result in a group that appreciates the library and its resources. The key to having a useful young adult program is to find a few people who show some genuine interest in the computer beyond playing arcade games. Participants can engage in the same activities as any other group of computer enthusiasts, including recreation, tutoring each other and swapping information and programming (here again, the same cautions about illegal copying of software apply).

It is important to have an adult sponsor who can suggest activities and who has enough knowledge to teach the fundamentals of computer literacy. Preferably, this person should be an outside volunteer, since most librarians won't have enough time to devote to such an endeavor.

To attract participants, try distributing fliers in schools, community halls and any other local gathering spot. A press release to local papers is also recommended, especially when seeking a sponsor. If you know of a community youth leader or counsellor who is looking for new ways of reaching young people who need direction, this type of library club may be an ideal vehicle.

Computer Reading Clubs

Computer reading clubs are one of the best ongoing activities a library can offer for children. They can be organized along the same lines as the traditional reading clubs sponsored by most libraries. Such clubs have the dual benefits of introducing children to computers while promoting reading at the same time. They can also be offered by libraries that do not have a public access micro (although having a micro on location will allow for more types of activities). A club devoted to reading about computers will certainly attract attention, but it must be managed properly if it is to achieve the desired objectives. Some guidelines for computer reading clubs follow.

1. Keep the club on a six-week schedule. A longer period of time may wear everyone out.

2. The goal of the whole effort should be to *introduce* children in the club to the computer. Each child will learn how to insert the diskette and will build an elementary vocabulary including such terms as "catalog," "diskette," "hardware," "software," "run," etc. Stay away from words like RAM or ROM. These concepts can be pursued with children who show interest in the computer when the club ends.

3. Keep the objectives clear. The club's main focus should be on reading, not learning to use the computer. Don't teach programming.

4. Plan some simple way to record the titles of the books each child reads. One method is to create a reading log for each child. This can contain additional materials such as bibliographies, puzzles (discussed below), appropriate software listings and the rules of the reading club.

Another way is to let children input their own titles into a data base at the computer Any good, easy-to-follow data base program can probably be used for this purpose. Or, if someone on the staff knows how to program, perhaps he or she can create a small data base system that the children can understand. (In this case, the program could also be customized to reflect whatever theme the library chooses for its reading club.) Periodically, a printout with a list of books read by the children can be displayed.

5. Establish goals for the children, so that they have an incentive to read more. Some clubs award "titles" to members based upon the number of books they have read, for example, "keypunch operator," "computer programmer," "systems analyst," etc. Another approach is to let the child become a "chip," "program," "monitor," "master control program," "disk drive" or "diskette." Be sure to work out a logical upward progression, so that children win more advanced titles as they read more.

6. Plan meetings to get the children together. Activities can include storytelling and having the children discuss the books they have read. Some fun with the computer should be planned, but not for the whole session. Suggestions include demonstrating simple, easy-to-run programs (chess, word games, elementary math, etc.) and various printout activities such as making calendars or individualized posters—children enjoy watching the computer work and having something to show their families. Also, look for films to enhance club meetings.

7. Use positive reinforcement. Anyone who reads at least one book should receive some form of recognition, such as a prize, a certificate or perhaps time to play a computer game on the library computer. Ask local computer stores if they will sponsor the club by contributing prizes.

8. Make an assortment of computer books available. No one should be forced to read particular computer books; just let the children know what books are available and where they are located.

9. Coordinate the program with a local school if possible.

10. Publicize the club to maintain interest in it. You can fix up a local display area in the library for participants' names and club information. Take a group picture of the top 10 or so "computer kids" and send it, along with a press release, to the local paper.

Outside Computer Clubs and User Groups

Many libraries have begun to provide outside microcomputer clubs or user groups with a meeting room on a regular basis. Sometimes this is in exchange for assistance with the library computer literacy program or other types of volunteer services. Having a club meet at the library can be a very good way to increase the pool of computer skills available for public access projects such as workshops or classes. To help find clubs in your area, consult *Computer Shopper*, a computer newspaper that gives national listings of computer clubs (see Appendix E).

If you provide space to outside clubs, make certain their members are aware of and adhere to all library rules, including those that pertain to use of the microcomputer (particularly in terms of copying software). Also, do not allow the club to monopolize the equipment.

Whether or not you provide space for outside clubs, it is a good idea to attend a local club meeting at least once. You can pass out any appropriate fliers or other materials about the library, and may find volunteers for your program. Keep in mind, however, that some club members may be local vendor representatives or programmers looking for a market for their software. These members will probably be more interested in selling their merchandise than in club activities and are not the best candidates for volunteers.

Library User Groups

A user group is one of the best ways for librarians to get together to share information. The number of library microcomputer user groups is increasing; however, library user groups devoted to public access are a relatively new phenomenon.

What may be the first public access user group for librarians started in Illinois in January 1983. Called the Public Access Microcomputer Users Group (PAMUG), the group sponsors regular talks on software and hardware, meeting at libraries which have public access equipment. "Planning and preparing to install public access equipment" was the theme of one meeting. Other meeting topics include bulletin board systems and a comparison of data base management systems. The group also publishes a newsletter, *PA Micro*. For information about the club, contact Ruth Griffith (who is credited with having initiated the group) at the Arlington Heights Memorial Library, 500 N. Dunton, Arlington Heights, IL 60004, (312) 392-0100.

A club not devoted strictly to public access is the Microcomputer Users Group for Libraries in North Carolina (MUGLNC), a statewide organization which publishes *News & Review*. MUGLNC has planned several successful and popular workshops for members. For more information, contact Duncan Smith, chairman of the steering committee, at Kernersville Branch Library, Forsyth County Public Library, 130 E. Mountain St., Kernersville, NC 27284, (919) 355-2632.

User groups are often formed for a particular brand of micro, but few of these are specifically for library users. One national group is the Apple Library Users Group (ALUG), formed by Monica Ertel of Apple Computer, Inc. The organization also publishes a newsletter and can be contacted care of Apple Computer Library, 20525 Mariani Ave. 18AJ, Cupertino, CA 95014.

The Public Library Association Microcomputer Task Force is in the process of compiling two microcomputer user data bases for libraries. One will be a file of existing library user groups; the other will maintain a list of users who are looking for others with whom they can form a user group. The application for inclusion in the data bases, called Library Microcomputer Users (formerly the Public Library Users Group), is shown in Figure 6.1. For further information, contact Barbara DeYoung, 51 Lawrence, Lawrence, MA 01840.

Figure 6.1: Library Microcomputer Users Application Form

```
                     LIBRARY MICROCOMPUTER USERS
                     DATABASE APPLICATION FORM



NAME:_____
TITLE:_____
LIBRARY:_____
TYPE: _____(PUBL) _____(ACAD) _____(SCHL) _____(SPEC)_____(OTHER)
STREET:_____
CITY:_____
STATE:_____ (TWO LETTER POSTAL CODE)      ZIP:_____
LIBRARY / ADMINISTRATIVE USE (Y/N):_____
PUBLIC ACCESS USE (Y/N):_____
ON-LINE DATABASE SEARCHING (Y/N):_____
CIRCULATING MICROCOMPUTERS (Y/N):_____

HARDWARE:  (LIST EACH TYPE OF MICROCOMPUTER)
NAME OF SYSTEM(S):_____
_____
OPERATING SYSTEM(S):_____
HARD DISK (Y/N):_____

SOFTWARE:
WORD PROCESSING (Y/N):_____      DATA MANAGEMENT (Y/N):_____
SPREADSHEET (Y/N):_____      COMMUNICATIONS (Y/N):_____
GAMES (Y/N):_____      EDUCATIONAL (Y/N):_____
USER DEVELOPED (Y/N):_____      INTEGRATED (Y/N):_____
UNIQUE ASPECTS OF YOUR SYSTEM / COMMENTS:_____
_____
_____
_____
```

GAME DAYS

Some libraries have established "Game Days" as a computer activity. These are primarily for children and often include arcade games. The theory is that allowing such periods once or twice each week will get the games "out of their system" as well as provide the library with some good will. A game day can last all day or for just a few hours. The library can set up game days on a regular basis or schedule them irregularly, for example, only on holidays. Keep in mind that game days are for high resolution or arcade games. Other types of games, such as text, math or chess, should not only be permitted on any day during regular appointments, but encouraged!

Exactly how such a program should be executed will depend upon the library and staffing arrangement. There should be sufficient space away from the normal flow of traffic. Anything that disrupts the normal activity of the library should be avoided. If appropriate space is not available, game days are probably not a good idea. Finally, no one needs to have an hour to play "Space Invaders," so limit the time to five minutes per person, more or less, and let children play in small groups of two or three.

As it turns out, by the way, children *don't* get games out of their system, they just want more. In a very short time, young people will be asking the staff, "When is the next game day?" As might be imagined, such events can drain the staff both mentally and physically (see the North-Pulaski discussion in Chapter 5).

Some guidelines for running game days are given below. The rules listed here are the result of my own observation and efforts at the North-Pulaski Library. Rules should be posted prominently in the library and near the computer.

1. A monitor is in charge of the computer and game area. Everyone must take instructions from this person.

2. No fighting, yelling, pushing or other unruly behavior will be tolerated. Anyone breaking this or other rules will be asked to leave the game area.

3. Games are selected by the monitor.

4. First come, first served. If too many people show up for game day, brief periods will be allowed for the number of people determined by the monitor.

If any type of game period is decided upon, be forewarned that, even if it is not heavily advertised, children spread the news very quickly and a crowd may show up. So where is the crowd put? If such a period lasts only a couple of hours, one option is to show movies for the children who are waiting their turn, assuming that the space and capability are available. Another is to schedule some sort of children's activity in conjunction with game day, in order to occupy those waiting their turn.

COMPUTER FAIRS

One very exciting event springing up in libraries everywhere is the computer fair, generally emphasizing software demonstrations. Fairs range from the extravaganza populated by dozens of vendors, to the simpler affairs with just a few participants. Local computer stores are usually happy to participate. Nearby or branch libraries with micro projects may also wish to attend to publicize their activities. Free hardware and software literature can often be obtained directly from the manufacturer for the asking. The demonstration of software programs is a vital part of any such event. "Running demos" of important programs such as VisiCalc can be obtained from a local vendor.

A slightly more involved project is the "Computer Month" concept. This entails numerous events over a period of weeks, including vendor demonstrations, workshops, special informational brochures, and any or all of the other activities described in this chapter. However, it takes an enormous amount of time to organize and coordinate such a project, especially if it is held in a large library system. Still, a well-organized project can be of tremendous benefit to system libraries, both in terms of enhancing their public image and by attracting new patrons.

One particularly noteworthy event of this type was the "Computer Fair" sponsored by the Lincoln Library in Springfield, IL, in April 1983. The fair lasted for four Saturdays. The first Saturday covered microcomputer basics such as hardware, software and selecting a computer. The second was devoted to specific applications such as word processing, education and inventory. The third concentrated on small business, examining such subjects as health services and client lists. The final Saturday covered miscellaneous topics including user groups, computer maintenance and support.

Each Saturday attracted 200 or more visitors, representing a broad range of ages. Vendors were present at several of the sessions. The event was publicized through the regular library bulletin, which is distributed to some 5000 families in Springfield, along with coverage in newspapers and other media.

OTHER SPECIAL EVENTS

There are many innovative special events that libraries can institute. Many of these are for children and most are one-time events, such as contests. The examples given below represent some of the imaginative ways libraries are using public access micros, or the theme of microcomputers, to attract patrons to the library.

Computer Parties

Many children's parties feature entertainment by a clown or magician. One innovative museum library came up with the idea of a "computer birthday party"[1] instead, held at the library. The birthday child and guests were entertained by playing educational computer games on the micro—the micro (an Atari) even gave a musical rendition of "Happy Birthday." The Oakville Public Library in Ontario, Canada, also has a birthday party program. For $3 per child, participants can use the computer for one hour. Groups are limited to eight to 10 children.

Libraries that are not able to accommodate regular birthday parties can still incorporate the micro into some of the yearly parties traditionally held. For example, if the library sponsors a Halloween party, it can let children play Haunted House (or another suitable computer game) at the micro in groups of three during the day.

Contests and Tournaments

Contests are a good way to stir up excitement among patrons and can be designed for any age level.

A good example is a programming contest. Participants compete with others in their age group. Each child, young adult or adult decides upon some special subject of his or her own choice and writes a program for it. It is a good idea to provide some simple games or utility programs that participants can use as examples, along with a brief handout of some basic words and instructions.

Young people often figure out how to write programs with a minimum of effort. Some older participants can even create a useful library tutorial or other type of program that the library can add to its collection. The library might want to specify that it gets a free copy of any program developed as part of the contest.

It's not necessary to have dozens of participants; if the contest attracts five or 10 contestants it should be considered a success. A programming contest can also be a good activity for a young adult micro club or other larger group.

Along the same lines, you can also hold a "Debugging Contest." Take a program that is in the public domain library collection and insert a bug (if it doesn't have one already). Put the defective copy on a diskette, and time the participants: the quickest one to debug the program wins.

Some libraries are experimenting with contests that use micros as their theme, but don't require actually using one. For example, the library can sponsor an art contest for children, using a variety of arcade game creatures as the subjects. Pac Man, a Space Invader or any other type of micro character will do. Children love to draw these characters in a thousand different variations. Many will create imaginative and appealing designs. The artwork can be judged and displayed in the same manner as for any other youth art exhibit.

Pac Man is a popular character for other types of contests as well. At the North Austin Branch of the Chicago Public Library, a "Pac Man Contest" was held as an incentive to get children to return their books on time. Each time children returned five books on time, they were allowed to put their names in a hat. The contest culminated in a drawing for a grand prize, an electronic Pac Man toy. A "Pac Kid of the Week" contest was created by the Parmlee Billings Library in Billings, MT, to encourage reading.[2] By reading books shown on a large game board, children help save "Pac Kid" from being overrun. Each week, a free game at the computer is provided for the winner.

Computer game tournaments are another popular activity. Instead of competing against each other in a game of chess, for example, players compete with the computer. Computer game tournaments can, however, be tricky to organize since traditional board games require more computer time than other types of games. Even a library with three or four computers will run into obstacles, since the higher levels of computer chess, backgammon or other games cannot be played in "real time," but may take hours—the computer does not execute a move until it has run through every possible combination. Providing lower levels of the game, especially for less experienced players, will eliminate this problem.

Game Master

The North-Pulaski Branch Library offers a unique activity for patrons: a free one-hour demonstration of an interactive game network called Gamemaster. Based in Evanston, IL, Gamemaster is the product of Harlow Stevens Jr. and Harlow Stevens Sr. Callers can interact with each other in a variety of ways including game playing, chatting and sending and receiving electronic mail. This takes place within the Gamemaster format, an electronic representation of a six-story Victorian mansion. For example, if a caller wishes to send an electronic letter, he or she enters the "Mail Room."

Though limited in scope—only six people at a time can connect to the network, which currently has only an Illinois access number—this service is interesting because of its unusual format and low cost. The basic membership fee is $10 and connect time costs $3 per hour. A free one-hour demonstration can be arranged by contacting Gamemaster, 1723 Howards St., Suite 219, Evanston, IL 60202, (312) 328-9009.

Gamemaster is a form of online service, a subject that will be explored more fully in Chapter 7.

Other Activities

Libraries should investigate using the microcomputer to enhance or create other activities as well—the possibilities are as unlimited as the imagination. For example, some children's librarians have begun to use the micro to supplement story hour with demonstrations or displays of appropriate software. This is recommended for small groups of 10 or less. At other libraries, including North-Pulaski, the computer is used to create word find or other types of puzzles. These are very popular with all age groups. MECC has various software which will create such puzzles. It also publishes *Activities for Computer Classes*, a manual that contains computer-related puzzles, worksheets and other activities.[3]

The library should also explore the possibility of having outside groups, such as scout troops, visit the library for a computer demonstration. For example, many troops now offer a "Computer Badge." If the groups are large, it will be necessary to schedule time and perhaps divide them up into smaller units of seven or less. A brief talk on what micros do and a demonstration of some simple programs can be followed by individual time at the computer.

CLASSES AND SEMINARS

Programs for Adults

Classes and seminars are the most appropriate activities to sponsor for adults. Generally speaking, classes should be limited to six weeks. Seminars are better because they are a one-shot deal, repeated as often as desired. They can also accommodate many more people than a six-week class. For most libraries, the amount of computer time available for each patron is limited. Therefore, it may be difficult to sponsor a programming class such as BASIC or ASSEMBLY—you may have a problem scheduling all of the people who want to practice or do homework for the class. A word processing or other type of seminar, on the other hand, should require little if any computer time since it relies on group demonstration, rather than individual work with the computer. It can also be a very effective way to serve the needs of patrons.

Word processing seminar given at the North-Pulaski Branch Library. Such programs are popular with adults.

A difficult part of either of these activities is finding the people to teach them. This in itself will limit the type of adult programming that can be attempted. Local small businesses will sometimes help by sending someone to teach a class or seminar in return for the publicity they receive as a result. Individual computer programmers—home hobbyists, student or college volunteers—will sometimes help as well. The library can, of course, consider hiring someone to put on a seminar.

Computer Assisted Instruction

Many libraries sponsor regular classes for patrons. Most often these are recreational classes, such as macrame or pottery, or continuing education or enrichment classes, such as English as a Second Language (ESL) or General Education Development (GED) programs. The classes are usually taught by volunteers or teachers from outside agencies.

Particularly for ESL or GED classes, the computer can be used to supplement the coursework. If feasible, computer time can be reserved for student use during the class period. If the library plans to offer this type of activity, it must work closely with the instructor in terms of software selection and scheduling.

The Groton (CT) Public Library has an information packet to be used by volunteer library instructors at the library. It includes an instructors manual and is available for $6.00 from Groton Public Library, Rte. 117, Groton, CT 06304.

Several libraries are also attempting to coordinate cooperative tutoring programs with local high schools. An example is the Sherman Park Branch of the Chicago Public Library (see Chapter 5).

PROMOTING ACTIVITIES

It often requires no effort at all to keep the library's public access micro occupied all the time. However, if the library depends solely on word of mouth, it may find that the micro is used primarily by children, playing mostly games. To appeal to a broad segment of the community, the first requirement is to have a well-balanced software collection (see Chapter 3). The second is to promote activities and services to all members of the community.

Press releases, newsletters, fliers and handouts can all be used to publicize the library's public access micro activities.[4] All are effective in attracting patrons, particularly adults. For example, all computer patrons at North-Pulaski are asked to fill out a brief "exit survey" after using the computer (see Figure 6.2). Recent results indicated that 29.9% heard about the program through either the newspaper or a flier.[5] This may account for the fact that 40% of all North-Pulaski computer users are over 21.[6]

In all promotional efforts, market the software, not the computer. Since many people do not yet know what a microcomputer can do, begin the educational process even before they call for an appointment. After sending an initial press release (see Chapter 5, Figure

Figure 6.2: North-Pulaski Exit Survey

```
PERSONAL COMPUTER CENTER SURVEY FORM - North-Pulaski Branch Library
4041 W. North Ave., Chicago, IL 60639     312-235-2727     The Chicago Public Library
```

1. Time in _____ Time Out _____
2. Programs used _____
   _____
   _____
   _____
3. Did you do any original programming?
   Yes _____ No _____
4. Ever take a computer course? _____
   Where? _____
5. Circle languages known...

   Fortran   BASIC   COBOL
   Pascal   Other _____

6. Major interest... Education _____
   Recreation _____ Business _____
   Other _____
7. How did you get to the Center?
   Public Trans _____ Car _____
   Walk _____

8. Did you bring any of your own programs? _____
9. Age group

   Under 12 _____
   12 to 20 _____
   20 to 30 _____
   30 to 50 _____
   50 to 60 _____
   60 or above _____

10. About how far away do you live?
    _____
11. Do you type? _____ How well? _____
    _____
12. Other comments _____
    _____
13. Is this your first time here?
    _____

5.1) to local papers or radio stations stating that a computer is at the library, follow it up with subsequent releases which focus on software and its use. An example of a follow-up release is given in Figure 6.3.

Announcements can be adjusted to suit specific library programs, but always appeal to people's needs. Do not assume that everyone understands the implications of a public access micro: That understanding may not exist.

Figure 6.3: Follow-up Publicity Announcement

FLASH!

Typing Tutor is now at the public library. This computer program can be used as a supplement to regular typing instruction or as a brushup for persons already skilled. The program will give instant feedback on computerized typing tests, as well as individualized practice on selected keys. Try it out. Call Jim at 333-3333 for a free one hour appointment.

Fliers

Fliers are a staple of all library promotional efforts and they are an effective way to promote micro services as well. Fliers can be distributed to patrons visiting the library and displayed in local schools, shopping centers, other institutions, train stations and just about any other place you can think of where people congregate. If your library system has a graphics department, perhaps it will help in creating a flier. If not, perhaps a volunteer or library staff member can do the job. Just be sure that the information given on the flier is complete, and that the service being promoted is the first thing to catch the eye (see Figure 6.4).

Handouts for Patrons

In addition to having a good supply of fliers on hand about various micro activities, the following will be appreciated by patrons:

1. A bibliography and checklist to aid in the purchase of a microcomputer. This will help patrons who are investigating computers to purchase. It should be updated at least once each year. If you work with a word processor, you can simply make corrections to the old version on diskette and print out the new copy.

2. Local computer clubs list. This can be compiled by the library. If there is a local paper that publishes club listings, it may save you the trouble of doing your own.

3. User's guide to the personal computer center. This can contain computer center and library rules, a software library catalog, a glossary, a description of the computer, and general information about the library. Include a bibliography, if desired. Do not include items that go out of date quickly.

Computer News Center

A good method of publicizing the computer within the library is to devote a regular bulletin board to the computer activities. The North-Pulaski board is labeled "Computer News Center." and it attracts and informs many patrons. All publicity, fliers and promotional literature about the computer are posted on it. This helps to generate the same type of interest as would a computer sitting in the open, but without the noise or risk. The word "computer" has powerful drawing power. If the board is maintained properly, people will be seen reading it thoughout the day.

The bulletin board can also be used as an information exchange. Encourage people with computer interests to list their specific need or service on the board. For example, if someone needs tutoring or help with specific computer programs a note to this effect can be posted. Create simple forms for patrons to fill out and post, or use blank three-by-five cards.

100   PUBLIC ACCESS MICROCOMPUTERS

Figure 6.4: North-Pulaski Promotional Flier

Have you read a good book lately? Share it with us on the Library Computer Bulletin Board System. The North-Pulaski Branch Library will feature book and movie reviews provided by librarians and non-librarians who contact us with their computer.

We would like your opinion about children's books, romances, adventure stories, westerns, computer technical manuals, or any other books you've read.

How about some "Social Comment?" The PMS is also a good place to voice your current thoughts about almost anything (within reason). Share your views with others; write your own editorials.

Messages and reviews are limited to 24 lines. PMS hours are generally 9 p.m. to 9 a.m., Monday through Thursday, 5 p.m. to 9 a.m., Friday and Saturday, and all day Sunday and Holidays. Call our computer at 235-3200.

The North-Pulaski Library is at 4041 W. North Avenue. The Center provides Apple Computer equipment free to the public during normal business hours by appointment only. Ask for Patrick R. Dewey, Librarian (voice 235-2727).

The PMS is a service of the Personal Computer Center which was made possible by a grant from the Friends of The Chicago Public Library.

(SEE REVERSE FOR INSTRUCTIONS)

Reprinted courtesy of the North-Pulaski Branch Library

The Computer News Center bulletin board at North-Pulaski.

Column in the Local Paper

Writing a regular monthly column for a local newspaper is something that few people have the time to do. However, this is a good way to increase the visibility of the microcomputer project and activities, and a way to help educate the general public about microcomputers in libraries. There are already many articles being written about microcomputers in general, so gear your column to use of the micro in your library. A few suggested topics include: computer services available in the library, a review of software available in the library, a general overview of the public access program, interviews with the people who use the computer or the staff who run the program, and what books the library has available about computers.

Newsletters

If you have the time to invest, a microcomputer newsletter to patrons can be an exciting and useful tool. North-Pulaski began such a publication, but found that it was soon impossible to print enough copies. When the mailing list reached 1000, the library ceased publication. Another alternative is to include micro center news in the library's regular newsletter. Topics should be software oriented. Include stories about successful patron projects and programs, and new software and equipment as they become available.

NOTES

1. Peter Hirshberg, "Compu-Tots and Other Joys of Museum Life," *Instructional Innovator* 26 (September 1981): 29.

2. " 'Pac Kid' Spurs Summer Reading in Billings, Montana," *LJ/SLJ Hotline* 11 (September 6, 1982): 4.

3. This is an excellent source of all types of computer activities, including puzzles. The worksheets can be reproduced and distributed to children who are awaiting their turn at the computer, or used to supplement computer club activities. It is available from the Minnesota Educational Computing Consortium, 2520 Broadway Dr., St. Paul, MN 55113. ($18. Publication #643).

4. For an in-depth treatment of these and other general library publicity techniques, see Benedict A. Leerburger, *Marketing the Library* (White Plains, NY: Knowledge Industry Publications, Inc., 1982).

5. The statistics were originally reported in Patrick R. Dewey, "Chicago, Illinois has Thriving Computer Center," *Library Journal* 107 (April 1, 1982): 674. The breakdown included: a friend, 30.05%; a librarian, 40.05%; a flier, 21.1%; a newspaper, 8.8%.

6. The statistics were originally reported in Patrick R. Dewey, "The Personal Computer Center at the North-Pulaski Library," *Educational Computer Magazine* 3 (March/April 1983): 29. Actual percentages included: 14% under 12; 46% from 12 to 21; and 40% over 21.

7

Electronic Bulletin Boards and Other Data Base Services

The management of groups of facts, or data bases, for direct use by patrons is not a new concept for librarians. However, the use of microcomputers to achieve this end allows for significant improvements not only in the types of information libraries can make available but in the ways patrons can access information. One example is the electronic bulletin board system (BBS), an online service that allows public access from the home via telephone. This chapter will describe the electronic bulletin board system and another new area of public access, permitting patrons to search remote data bases such as The Source, BRS After Dark and others. The chapter concludes with a brief discussion of library-produced (or local) data bases, such as the curio file and wall charts for reference.

ELECTRONIC BULLETIN BOARD SYSTEM

The electronic bulletin board system (BBS) is an example of both a library-produced data base and an online service. The first known board was tested by Ward and Christensen in 1978.[1] The concept has caught on and a variety of systems have been developed. At least a thousand BBSs are currently in operation in the United States for all kinds of applications. Stores, clubs and individuals all operate boards for dissemination of information, distribution of public domain software, entertainment applications and more.

Library experience with the BBS is considerably smaller. Gene and Marion Wilburn began operating a bulletin board for librarians in Ontario, Canada, in 1981.[2] Called INFOPORT, the system, which operated on a TRS-80 micro, featured news and articles about different types of microcomputer applications in Ontario libraries. INFOPORT ceased operation in March 1983. A fledgling operation has just begun at the Waukegan (IL) Public Library and is run by volunteers. The only public access system operated and field-tested by librarians continuously for several years is the People's Message System (PMS) at the North-Pulaski Branch Library.* The PMS is therefore used as an example throughout this chapter.

What is a BBS?

Simply put, a BBS is the online version of a traditional bulletin board. It is a small data base program that is usually operated on a microcomputer. (Some larger systems run on mini and mainframe computers, but these are not considered here.) Like the traditional bulletin board, an electronic BBS is "blank" until information is entered into it by users or by the system operators.

There are a variety of bulletin board programs available for most major microcomputers (see Appendix F). They differ in the way they are structured: some allow only messages, others can accommodate messages, short articles and announcements, still others can allow interactive games to be played. The amount of information that can be entered by the system operator and callers is determined by the disk space available.

Depending upon the type of bulletin board program selected, people who are signed on can perform any of the following functions:

1. Read and leave messages (a form of electronic mail).

2. Read feature material (articles).

3. Download public domain computer programs.

4. Play games while online.

Usually, one particular board cannot accommodate all of these functions. Of them, reading and leaving messages is the principal reason that people call a BBS. At North-Pulaski, the first three functions are available. Although the last, game playing, is a feature of many commercial BBSs, it was never one of our purposes and is not recommended for any library.

The number of potential uses for a BBS is practically as endless as the number of microcomputer uses. Essentially, a board can be tailored to suit a special interest (such as users of a particular brand of micro), an activity (such as chess) or a general purpose.

---

*A predecessor of the PMS at North-Pulaski was the Apple Bulletin Board System (ABBS), inaugurated in 1981. The ABBS was abandoned in early 1983, mainly because of system crashes and other maintenance problems.[3]

How a BBS Operates

Like all other online services, a BBS requires a modem. As explained in Chapter 1, a modem is a device that allows digital codes to be sent and received over the analog telephone lines. It allows communication between your micro and any other micro, network or mainframe system so equipped. The rate or speed at which this communication occurs is called *baud*. The usual baud rate for a BBS is 300, or 30 characters per second—less than the speed at which most people read. A deeper understanding of these devices is not really necessary; just keep in mind that they are needed for any type of online telecommunications service.

Of the two types of modems available, acoustic and direct connect, a direct connect modem is essential for the operation of a BBS. It will eliminate at least one source of problems, extraneous noise. Modems operate at 300 or 110 baud, and most, if not all, can adjust to match the baud rate of a caller's modem. Only one person can call up and connect with the bulletin board at any one time.

Some may feel that the number of patrons with modems is too small to warrant attempting such a service, but this is not the case. There are now thousands of people with a modem in any major metropolitan area, and they are one of the most enthusiastic groups of patrons to be found. In fact, one comment often repeated on the North-Pulaski board is that callers are very happy to find a library providing such a service. They are tired of the commercial systems available, which are primarily technical or game boards, and appreciate the variety that a library BBS provides.

In December 1983 alone, the North-Pulaski system received 1017 calls. As of February 1984 the system had received more than 10,000 calls since its inception. Approximately 50% of the callers are from outside Chicago, and 2% are from out of state. As the proliferation of home computers continues, the pool of users will increasingly resemble the usual patron base of libraries.

Signing On

When patrons sign on to the North-Pulaski bulletin board, the first thing they are asked for is a user identification code (USERID), a seven-digit password. Passwords are assigned by the library, at the patron's request. For patrons without a password, several questions such as name, address and telephone number are requested for the logfile. Once this information is entered, the patron is logged in and given the greeting and opening message.

At North-Pulaski, passwords are used only for convenience. Some private boards require a password in order to enter the system, but since the North-Pulaski board is for public access, this is not the case. Patrons can leave a request for a password on the BBS. If a password has not been used by the patron for several months, it is cancelled, since it requires disk space to maintain.

When the patron signs on, the computer enters the proper name, address and other log-on information, as well as the proper terminal parameters (e.g., clear screen characters, parity, etc.). After logging on, the patron can choose to view a variety of options, including feature articles supplied by the system operator (SYSOP), or the message files that are created by each caller. Figure 7.1 is an example of what would appear on the screen once a user logs on to the North-Pulaski BBS. The opening message information changes from time to time as the library's requirements change.

Figure 7.1: Opening Message Display

```
GOOD EVENING PATRICK!
LOGGING CALL  # 8202 ON 12/30/83 AT 19:03


THE APPLE COMPUTER USED IN THIS PROGRAM
WAS OBTAINED WITH A GENEROUS GRANT FROM
THE FRIENDS OF CHICAGO PUBLIC LIBRARY


TYPE N FOR SYSTEM NEWS
TYPE F  FOR FEATURES MENU
TYPE NEWCALL IF YOUR FIRST CALL
TYPE H FOR HELP
TYPE S FOR PAUSE
        -ANY OTHER KEY TO CONTINUE
TYPE K TO STOP OUTPUT AND GO TO
        NEXT FUNCTION


NOTE: THERE IS A 45 MINUTE TIME LIMIT
FOR EACH CALL.


TYPE G FOR GOODBY—PLEASE DO NOT EXIT
BY SIMPLY RESETTING OR HANGING UP

TYPE ?  FOR A MENU OF COMMANDS

     Command: E,F,G,H,I,K,M,N,O,Q,QP
              R,RP,S, SP, T, U, X,?*$
```

Experienced users can eliminate the command prompts by typing in X, for expert. For users who become confused, extensive HELP files are available. Some patrons download or transfer this information to their computer or to hard copy and review it at their leisure.

Reading Messages

The message base is accessed by entering R, for "read message." The North-Pulaski BBS holds up to 75 messages. Messages are automatically deleted, the oldest first, as new messages accumulate—an important feature for any BBS system. The size of the message base is determined by the amount of disk space available. The system operator determines the maximum length of messages—on the North-Pulaski BBS callers can leave messages of up to 21 lines.

Patrons can determine which messages are worth reading by typing in the SP command. This allows users to scan message headers or subject lines. Messages can be scanned backward or forward, beginning at any number by typing in a plus (+) or minus (-) sign. A partial message scan as it would appear on the screen is shown in Figure 7.2.

Figure 7.2: Partial Message Scan

```
Msg# 2330 on 12/20/83 @22:06 (13)
Subj: ONLINE SEARCHING, To: (Patron name deleted)
From: Sysop

Msg# 2331 on 12/20/83 @22:11 (18)
Subj: LOGON IDs, To: ALL
From: Sysop

Msg# 2332 on 12/20/83 @22:16 (10)
Subj: HOURS OF THIS BOARD, To: ALL
From: Marvin Garber

Msg# 2336 on 12/21/83 @07:58 (4)
Subj: EDUCATORS BBS, To: ALL (educators)
From: (Patron name deleted)

Msg# 2337 on 12/21/83 @20:39 (9)
Subj: EXTENDED BOARD HOURS, To: ALL
From: Marvin Garber

Msg# 2350 on 12/23/83 @23:16 (7)
Subj: LIBRARY, To: (Patron name deleted)
From: (Patron name deleted)

Msg# 2351 on 12/24/83 @22:34 (7)
Subj: FRIENDS OF LIBRARY, To: SYSOP
From: (Patron name deleted)

Msg# 2352 on 12/24/83 @23:46 (6)
Subj: LIBRARY, To: (Patron name deleted)
From: (Patron name deleted)

Msg# 2388 on 12/29/83 @10:10 (1) <Pvt>
Subj: YOUR REQUEST, To: (Patron name deleted)
From: Sysop

Msg# 2390 on 12/29/83 @21.13 (9)
Subj: NEED HELP, To: COMMODORE 64 USERS
From: (Patron name deleted)

Msg# 2398 on 12/30/83 @07:18 (9)
Subj: COMPUTADORA !, To: (Patron name deleted)
From: (Patron name deleted)
```

Other commands available include the SR, or search command. Using this command, a caller can limit the search through the various message headers to a specific item, such as "book." If a caller enters the SR command and specifies the item "book," he or she can quickly retrieve any messages with the word "book" in their "subject" lines. The R command allows the user to read the messages one at a time or to read an entire sequence at once. An actual message from the board is illustrated in Figure 7.3.

Figure 7.3: Sample Message

```
Command: $R2390

Msg# 2390 on 12/29/83 @21.13 (9)
Subj: NEED HELP, To: COMMODORE 64 USERS
From: Patron name deleted, Chicago, IL

All Commodore 64 users leave phone numbers and names in order to be in contact with others for
future reference or help when you need it. There will be a list of names and phones if you call XXX-
XXXX in Chicago only. Let's make it easy. We all need your help. Leave all information To: (Patron
Name Deleted) in this board or call if you want. Every Commodore 64 user will thank you for your
interest. This is the "OPERATION HELP" as you read it on other boards. Thanks again.

End msg #2390
```

Feature Articles

The feature articles are accessed by typing F, for Features. A list of current articles online, along with the specific code for the corresponding file, is displayed. An example of accessing feature articles is shown in Figure 7.4. As mentioned earlier, the number and length of feature articles is determined by the disk space available. In the North-Pulaski BBS, about 100 double-spaced screens of feature information can be accommodated.

Only the system operator can post feature articles on the board. At North-Pulaski, articles that are submitted by patrons, librarians or others are first edited, then entered into the system. It is a good idea to involve the staff and volunteers in the writing of articles. As with a newsletter, invite callers and staff to contribute recipes, book or movie reviews, or articles on any other subject that people may find interesting.

Do something to make the board unique or different from other boards. Do not attempt to create all of the files yourself. A good editor gets others to generate the raw material. Those who contribute to the files should be informed if there are any favorable comments regarding their work. You might also ask local libraries if they want to participate in a cooperative public information effort. The service will repay the cost of time involved in good public relations alone.

Figure 7.4: Feature Articles Display

```
Comand: $F

Format for printer (Y/N)?:N

Special Features & Articles


We welcome suggestions for new features. Anyone who can contribute a regular column or an occasional paper should contact us at 235-2727 during the day. Ask for Pat or Marv. Thanks!


BOOKS = Book Sales at the Chicago Public Library
        (This feature will resume in 1984.)

BBS = Local Bulletin Board Systems

CPL = Chicago Public Library/Chicago Library System

CPL-S = La Biblioteca Publica de Chicago

CLUBS = Computer clubs

CARC = Computer Assisted Reference Center

ED = Directory of MicroEducation in Chicagoland

FOOD = Recipes from "Arminee & Friends"

JUV = Puzzles, games and news for the kids

LAW = State's Attorney's Office Services

LEARN = Study Unlimited video learning program

MICRO = Library microcomputer services/locations in Chicago

PCC = Basic facts about the Personal Computer Center

PETS = To your Pet's Good Health:  A monthly feature

PLATO = PLATO interactive learning-training computer

PROGI = Download Instructions

PROG1 = Download "I Dare You" (Important: Integer Program!)

PROG2 = Download "Quest" Adventure Game

PROG3 = Download "Stars" Elementary Guessing Game
```

Downloading from the BBS

In January 1984 a new feature was added to the North-Pulaski BBS: allowing patrons to download software to their own computers over the telephone. Surprisingly, it was far easier to accomplish this than we had imagined.

All of the programs that are made available are in the public domain. Since North-Pulaski has hundreds of such public domain programs, we attempt to put up whatever we have disk space for. If the programs are short, we put up more; if they are long, we put up fewer. If the regular feature articles happen to take up more space than usual, we enter smaller or fewer public domain programs. On the North-Pulaski BBS, programs available for downloading appear under the heading "PROG" in the features display (see Figure 7.4).

Anyone calling from anywhere in the country can access these programs, as long as they have a computer, a modem and a telecommunications or terminal software package, such as ASCII Express, that will allow them to capture the data. Even without such a package, some patrons can still print the program out in hard copy, type it back into their computer and run it out again as a program. This is a tedious task, but a surprisingly large number of people seem to want to do it.

The software offered for downloading on the North-Pulaski BBS covers a wide range of topics, including utility programs, games and educational programs. Download instructions are also available online. They are reproduced as they appear on the screen in Figure 7.5.

Figure 7.5: Download Instructions on the North-Pulaski BBS

Download Instructions

You will probably need a "terminal package" to "Download" programs from this PMS. ASCII Express, for example, works very well.

Once the file (PROG1, PROG2, or PROG3) has been loaded into your RAM, write the file to disk. Later—use the "EXEC" command, an Apple DOS command (explained more fully on page 78 of the Apple II DOS manual), to then LOAD the text file back into the Apple as an Apple program. Then SAVE it as you would any Apple program. It should RUN. Make sure that you SAVE it in the correct LANGUAGE—either Applesoft or Integer. (Integer programs are clearly labelled as such in the "F" file on this board.) Some programs will not work in both languages.

It is entirely possible that, since many of the programs are simple BASIC, some callers who do not have Apple Computers may wish to attempt to download them and perform the conversion necesary to make them run on other machines. Good luck!

If you have any public domain programs that we could post for the benefit of others, please let us know. Call us at 235-2727 (voice). Ask for Pat Dewey or Marvin Garber.

Finally, please, please, please let us know of any problems so that we might correct them.

We appreciate your help. Thanks!

Pat & Marv

SELECTING A BBS

Before investigating which bulletin board system to purchase, you should become familiar with one and with other aspects of online communications. A good source of information is *The Complete Handbook of Personal Computer Communications*, by Alfred Glossbrenner. This book gives a comprehensive view of microcomputer telecommunications possibilities. Topics covered include the electronic bulletin board, networks, hardware, software and other information.

Probably the best way to learn about bulletin board systems is to access one. It is preferable to have someone knowledgeable in their use to show you how, but you can manage on your own, if necessary. The following libraries are operating bulletin board systems as of this writing (the numbers listed are for accessing the boards):

North-Pulaski Branch Library PMS: (312) 235-3200
Waukegan (IL) Public Library BBS: (312) 623-2226

You can also call any one of the many commercial boards in operation. Next, get literature about all of the bulletin board programs that are available. Appendix F lists bulletin board software sources.

The important things to consider when looking for a board include ease of use (some boards require a great deal of technical skill), ease of maintenance, reliability, hardware requirements, adequate documentation and backup support. These selection criteria are discussed in more detail below.

1. A BBS should first and foremost have excellent *error-trapping*; it should be able to recover quickly from user input errors, not go down every time a user hits the wrong key. This was the major reason that North-Pulaski eventually dropped the ABBS program in favor of the PMS.

2. The board should be *information oriented*. Make sure that the program format allows for the convenient addition of SYSOP-created files, in addition to letting users read and leave messages. Files generated by the library staff will allow the posting of library-related events and activities. Many people may be attracted to a technological innovation, but without regular attractions and useful information, they are unlikely to consider the BBS a place to call regularly. In other words, make it perform the basic library function of information distribution.

3. The board should be *easy to use*. Documentation and HELP files should be clear and easy to follow and should contain a healthy section on problems. If patrons have difficulty figuring out what to do, they simply won't call back.

4. Make sure that the program can be *easily backed up*. If a system cannot be easily backed up on a daily basis, it should not be considered. (System back up is discussed further under "Upkeep," below.)

5. There should be some *local support*. If you cannot find a local dealer, then at least make contact with someone who has been running a board like the one you want to install *before* you purchase it. Most local SYSOPs are happy to lend a hand. Ask how much time it requires to operate and how much technical skill is needed. Explain your current situation (e.g., how much you know about computers).

6. Check out the *hardware requirements*. Do you have all the proper equipment to make the board work? Some manufacturers—PMS, for example—will send you the diskettes already configured for your system if you tell them what equipment you have in advance.

7. Investigate the type of *password arrangement* the system has. As noted earlier, some boards are private, requiring a password to access. This is an advantage for professional networking, but not particularly suitable for public access. Others, such as Net-Works, allow for a private board within a public board; the second board is restricted to people who possess a special password. Thus you can have one board for the public and one for librarians. Anyone can access the first, but only librarians can access and leave messages on the second.

8. Before making any decision to purchase, *talk to another BBS operator who has been running a board for a while.*

UPKEEP OF THE BBS

A bulletin board system requires a certain amount of daily maintenance to run properly. This involves housekeeping tasks, such as clearing the log file and bringing the system "down" (i.e., clearing it) each day, along with priming the board with articles or new features, if needed. Many of these tasks can be done by part-time staff members or volunteers.

The log file is a record of callers to the BBS. The information in it is available only to the system operator. It can be accessed at the micro in the library or from home, using the system password (not to be confused with the caller password).

The log file has several useful and interesting functions. It serves as a record of calls received, provides statistics on the calls and contains the phone numbers of people who have requested a password. Figure 7.6 shows a partial log file display as it appears on the North-Pulaski BBS (all patron names are fictitious).

The North-Pulaski BBS program allows us to check the average amount of time spent on the system by callers. Statistics recorded in December 1983 indicated that of 92 consecutive callers, the average call was 15 minutes in duration. Only 12 callers stayed online for less than five minutes. This statistic shows that callers are staying on long enough to browse through our various departments. We also find that many people call back on a regular basis.

It may take 10 minutes to an hour each morning to take the system "down." In

Figure 7.6: North-Pulaski Log File Display

```
Comand: $LOGFILE
```

Name of caller	City/State	Phone	Date	Time	#
*Patrick Dewey	Chicago, IL	235-2727	12/30/83	16:21:27	8194
Eric Freeden	Lisle, IL	XXX-7354	12/30/83	17:07:06	8195
Jim Kalerski	Chicago, IL	NONE	12/30/83	17:45:53	8196
Boyd Babcock	Salt Lake City, UT	801-XXX-2854	12/30/83	17:33:41	8197
Dave Howard	Chicago, IL	XXX-7858	12/30/83	17:45:14	8198
*Bill Barden	Chicago, IL	XXX-3984	12/30/83	18:40:12	8199
*Marvin Garber	Chicago, IL	235-2727	12/30/83	18:51:12	8200

CPL/N-P BBS LOGFILE FOR 12/30/83 (7 ENTRIES)
Delete file $Y

Note: On the North-Pulaski BBS, an asterisk before a caller's name indicates that the caller used a password.

addition to reading the log file, this involves running off messages when necessary and responding to them. At night, inserting the diskettes to boot the system, or prepare it for running, should take only five minutes or so. Make sure that the system will automatically return to normal (autoboot) without human intervention in the event of a power failure.

Backing up the diskettes each day is the most important part of maintaining a good system. A BBS program diskette is subjected to heavy and continuous use. Therefore, the program must be transferred to a new diskette each day to prevent diskette failure. The North-Pulaski BBS is backed up six times each week. There are six sets of backup diskettes plus a working or master copy.

SYSTEM FAILURE

Having a system fail is frustrating, especially if you cannot determine why it failed or how to prevent a similar failure in the future. While no system can be completely safeguarded, there are a number of steps you can take to reduce the chances of a system crash.

Common causes of system failure include equipment overheating, dirty connectors, disk failure, power surges and mischievous users who break into the system. To counteract these, the following steps are recommended:

1. Install a fan to prevent overheating.

2. Clean the computer regularly with the recommended methods. Often, an ordinary pencil eraser can be used to clean connectors.

3. Back up diskettes frequently and replace working diskettes every three months.

4. Install a surge protector, if necessary.

5. Use a unique system password. Never associate it with something that can be easily guessed, such as a name.

6. Always check that you have remembered to plug the telephone line back in after disconnecting it for maintenance—a surprisingly common reason why a system won't work!

OBSCENITY AND SECURITY PROBLEMS

Most of the people who call the library BBS will be legitimate users, but there are always a few who will abuse any public service. One answer to the "four letter word syndrome" is to install an Obscenity Filter (this comes as standard equipment on the North-Pulaski BBS program, the PMS). This is a program feature that automatically checks each message against an operator-defined file of undesirable words. If the message contains one, it is refused. Obviously, a determined user can misspell a word slightly and circumvent the filter, but such occurrences are rare. In a year of operation at North-Pulaski, only one such incident took place.

There are other steps that you can take to discourage "system crashers" or "phreaques," as they are sometimes called. Most important, do not engage in any discussion or response on the board. If the message is threatening, file a report with the police. Finally, contact the telephone company and urge an investigation each time an incident occurs. At North-Pulaski, we also post a standard censorship message periodically (see Figure 7.7).

The most important aspect of system security is to guard the system password files. As mentioned earlier, these should be unique. In addition, if volunteers work on the system and have access to passwords and other confidential information, make certain that they sign a nondisclosure agreement.

Figure 7.7: North-Pulaski BBS Censorship Message

```
Subj: Censorship   To: All
From: SYSOP

What is our policy on censorship on this board?

We would like to say that we do not believe in censorship, and follow the American Library Association policy of resisting it wherever it is threatened. There are, however, certain laws and regulations governing use of the telephone lines. We do not, therefore, censor messages on this board except under what we hope are rare circumstances, such as in the case of outright obscenities, illegal activity such as piracy, slander, or a gross breach of good taste. We believe you will agree, if you have read much of what has appeared here, that we have applied very liberal standards, and have used great restraint.
```

PUBLIC ACCESS TO REMOTE DATA BASES

As we have seen, interest is growing in public access data bases and online services such as the bulletin board system. As more and more libraries establish public access microcomputers equipped with telecommunications links, attention may turn to an area that has remained, for the most part, uncharted: public access to remote data bases, or online services.

This is an exciting area of public access service, but it raises many questions. First, commercial online services such as The Source, CompuServe, BRS and others charge for each use of their data bases. This means that libraries will either have to absorb the cost or pass it along to patrons. This escalates the question of "fee or free" that libraries are still grappling with regarding information searches conducted for patrons.

If a library does decide to pass costs along to patrons, it will have a difficult time determining what those costs are. The online services charge for connect time and for the amount of time spent in each data base (each data base has differing rates). The library would either have to rely on patrons to provide this information, or stay with the patron for the entire time. Neither solution is practical. One possibility is to offer such services to patrons who wish to open an account with The Source, Dialog or other networks but don't have a microcomputer at home. All charges would then automatically appear on the patron's account and the library would only have to pay the cost of the local phone call. This, of course, would limit such services to those who can pay for them, giving rise to a fresh area for debate.

Second, allowing patrons to access online services directly calls into question the need for librarians as search intermediaries—another area of controversy. Obviously, these are issues that go beyond the scope of this book. However, we suggest here that, just as these difficulties have not prevented libraries from offering search services, they will not prevent the growth of public access to those services. With this in mind, we turn to a brief discussion of several online consumer networks that libraries may consider.

CONSUMER NETWORKS

CompuServe, The Source, Dow Jones News/Retrieval Service, Dialog Information Services and Bibliographic Retrieval Services (BRS) all offer non-prime time (generally evenings and weekends) access to their services at a reduced cost from their prime time or business day rates. The services are marketed specifically to the home computer user. The consumer version of the Dialog service is called Knowledge Index; BRS calls its service BRS After Dark. These networks offer online programs, hobbyist services, shopping by computer, electronic mail, "chat," and hundreds of other services.

The Source and CompuServe offer the greatest variety of services oriented toward the consumer. It is likely that the average public library will have many more patrons who will be attracted to these services than those who want to work with the bibliographic data bases offered by BRS After Dark and Knowledge Index, or the primarily specialized financial services offered by Dow Jones News/Retrieval.

Typical sessions on all these systems begin with the user accessing the system through either Tymnet or Telenet, or a special WATS telephone line. Telephone charges generally equal only the cost of a local telephone call. Connect time charges can vary, depending upon the time of day the call is made and, sometimes, the baud rate used. Higher baud rates often mean a higher price. When different rates are offered to the subscriber, the cheapest rates are always in the evenings (non-prime time), the most expensive during the business day (prime time).

The Source and CompuServe

CompuServe and The Source offer the user a wide range of services including the ability to make airline reservations, get weather reports from around the country, shop for books or just about anything else and, of course, send electronic mail. The number and types of services change very quickly during the course of the year. The printed user manuals become obsolete almost before they are published and their format changes rapidly. Apparently, these services—most notably, The Source—cannot decide how to best document their systems.

There is a strong leaning toward leisure-type activities on these systems, since many of the services are constructed with the home or recreational computer user in mind. The CB Simulation on CompuServe is a good example. In this mode of operation, the user can talk or "chat" with others online in much the same manner as one would use a CB radio. The Source has a regular "chat" service. Anyone online can attempt to get the attention of anyone else online and carry on a "keyboard conversation," regardless of where the other person is located.

Another popular service on these systems is the user directory. On The Source, subscribers can input their first name, state, major interests (e.g., computers) and USERID into this directory for others to search. The file contains hundreds of such entries. If you find someone who has similar interests, you can just drop that person an electronic letter. The networks have their own bulletin board systems and also have a list of national electronic bulletin board systems. Users can post their own notices on the bulletin board systems of these services—for example, we have advertised the North-Pulaski BBS by posting the information and number in the system; several people have called as a result.

Futurists have long theorized that such services will eventually replace traditional mail services. However, that is still a long way off. These electronic services are by subscription only; therefore, it is impossible to send instant letters to people who have not subscribed or to people who have subscribed to a different service. Furthermore, if the person to whom a letter was sent accesses the system infrequently, the "instant" letter might not be received for weeks. Greater technological sophistication does not necessarily mean greater efficiency!

Knowledge Index and BRS After Dark

Knowledge Index and BRS After Dark differ from The Source and CompuServe in that they offer access to bibliographic data bases. The number of data bases offered is much less than what is offered on the daytime (prime time) counterparts, Dialog Information Retrieval Service and BRS. In early 1984 Knowledge Index offered 21 data bases and BRS After Dark offered 29 data bases. As with The Source and CompuServe, changes occur very rapidly on these services, with data bases being added or deleted on a monthly—sometimes weekly—basis, depending upon subscriber interests.

As of early 1984, the data bases offered on Knowledge Index included Books in Print, National Technical Information Service (NTIS), National Newspaper Index (NNI), ABI/Inform, Standard & Poor's News and Microcomputer Index, to name a few. Among those offered on BRS After Dark were Biosis Previews, CA Search, MEDLINE, Harvard Business Review/Online, *Academic American Encyclopedia* and PsycINFO. BRS After Dark also offers electronic mail (in conjunction with MCI).

Dow Jones News/Retrieval Service

The Dow Jones News/Retrieval Service does not offer the bibliographic data bases offered on BRS After Dark and Knowledge Index. Like The Source and CompuServe, it offers electronic mail services (in conjunction with MCI), a shop-at-home service called Compu-Store, movie reviews, weather and news reports. In addition, users can access specialized financial services including Dow Jones Business and Economic News, Dow Jones Quotes (stocks) and Financial and Investment Services. Dow Jones News/Retrieval also offers the *Academic American Encyclopedia* online.

Start-up fees, rates, range of service, hours of operation and other information are summarized for each of these networks in Table 7.1. All information is as of early 1984, but readers are urged to contact each vendor for the most up-to-date information.

Library Experience with Online Services

In actual practice, few libraries seem to have made such services available to their patrons, possibly because of the difficulties discussed earlier. One successful effort has been with the online *Academic American Encyclopedia*, offered through BRS After Dark and Dow Jones News/Retrieval Service.[4] This service was first offered to students at the Princeton (NJ) High School Library. The library mainly uses Dow Jones News/Retrieval to access the encyclopedia, possibly because Dow Jones offers a discount to academic institutions (the company is also located in Princeton). Some 200 school and university libraries now offer the *Academic American Encyclopedia* online to their students.

CompuServe undertook a similar effort with the *World Book Encyclopedia*, but it was discontinued when the publisher dropped out of the project. Unfortunately, even though many students seem eager to use these resources, online encyclopedias leave much to be desired when compared with the richness of traditional books. None offers pictures along with text, and there is also no way to browse in the data base. Not all of these online encyclopedias offer the user the ability to search the full text ("free text" search). Some can only be accessed by article title.

Table 7.1: Comparison of Online Consumer Networks*

Name	Start-up Charge	Service	Monthly Fee or Minimum	Cost	Baud	Hours
BRS After Dark 1200 Rt 7 Latham, NY 12110 (800) 833-4707	$50	29 data bases, electronic mail, online encyclopedia	$12	$6/hr.	300 1200	M-F: 6pm-3am Sat: 6am-4am Sun: 6am-2pm 7pm-4am
CompuServe 5000 Arlington Centre Blvd. Columbus, OH 43220 (800) 848-8199	$40	news, shop-at-home, "chat," electronic mail, games, etc.	None	$6/hr. $12/hr.	300 1200	M-F: 6:01pm-4am weekends, holidays
				$12.50/hr. $15/hr.	300 1200	M-F: 8am-6pm
Dow Jones News/Retrieval (standard service) Dow Jones & Co. PO Box 300 08540 Princeton, NJ 08540 (800) 257-5510	$75	financial news and investment services, stock quotes, electronic mail, online encyclopedia	None	$0.15/min. up $0.30/min. up	300 1200	M-F: 6:01pm-4am weekends, holidays
				$0.40/min. up $0.80/min. up	300 1200	M-F: 6am-6pm
Knowledge Index Dialog Information Services, Inc. 3460 Hillview Ave. Palo Alto, CA 94304 (800) 227-5510	$35	21 data bases	None	$24/hr. $24/hr.	300 1200	M-Th: 6pm-5am F: 6pm-12am Sat: 8am-12am Sun: 3pm-5am
The Source 1616 Anderson Rd. McLean, VA 22102 (800) 336-3330	$100	news, shop-at-home, "chat," electronic mail, games, etc.	$10	$7.75/hr $10.75/hr.	300 1200	M-F: 6:01pm-7am, weekends, holidays
				$20.75/hr. $25.75/hr.	300 1200	M-F: 7am-6pm

*All information and prices are as of January 1984.

At the Oakville Public Library in Canada, where some 14 microcomputers are in use, The Source is used in the evening hours (after 6 p.m.) by children in the 5th to 8th grades. Initial reports indicate that the children use the online systems with considerable ease.[5]

LOCAL DATA BASES

It may be some time before libraries begin offering patrons the ability to search consumer data bases directly. However, libraries can make local data bases available for public access. These can be library-produced data bases or prepackaged files available from vendors. Both are discussed briefly below.

Library-produced Data Bases

Many libraries maintain a card file, or curio file, of facts or data that are frequently referred to by patrons. These are generally short-answer or ready-reference types of information. Librarians can use the microcomputer to "automate" these files and organize them into data bases. Patrons can access the information much more easily in this form than when it is kept in traditional paper files.

Any number of data bases can be constructed. Libraries can produce files on career opportunities, educational institutions, community organizations, scholarships—in short, on any subject of continuing interest to patrons. One specialized project, undertaken at the Chicago Public Library, was the Native American Information and Referral Center. This library-produced data base contained organizations and agencies, along with names and numbers, that aided the Native American community.

Prepackaged Files

If a library cannot produce its own data base, it should investigate the availability of prepackaged files. For example, the Coordinated Occupational Information Network (COIN), available from Bell & Howell, is in place at several locations in the Chicago Public Library. For use with the Apple computer, the system allows the patron to search in a variety of ways for occupational and educational data. Included are files devoted to school subjects, careers, college majors, colleges and universities, apprenticeships and military service. An "interest profile" helps match the user to occupations by interest, working conditions, career clusters, educational levels, physical strengths, physical demands and salary range. Patrons can access the material using a microcomputer. The material is also available on microfiche.

Wall Charts

A second type of data base is the wall chart for patron reference. Although this is not an example of patron use of the computer, it is nonetheless a type of public access service, and one that would not be possible to provide without a microcomputer.

Two types of wall charts have been produced at North-Pulaski—the Subject Guide Wall Chart and the Software Wall Chart. Both are popular with patrons and are tremendous time-savers, as well.

The groundwork for the Subject Guide Wall Chart began several years ago at North-Pulaski. To save time in answering patron reference questions, we began to maintain a list of the most frequently asked for subject headings along with their corresponding Dewey Decimal and Library of Congress (LC) numbers. The list was kept at the reference desk. Eventually, we converted the list into a data base using the public access Apple computer and The Data Factory program.

From this data base, we produced a printout of 558 headings with corresponding

Dewey and LC numbers (see Figure 7.8). The printout (which is is updated occasionally) is mounted on a poster board and laminated. The cost to produce the chart was $10, including labor. Without a microcomputer, this project could not have been undertaken, since the time and labor required to make and update the chart manually would be prohibitive.

The chart is self-explanatory and patrons rarely need assistance when using it. Also, unlike other reference aids, such as COM catalogs, wall charts do not require maintenance (except for an occasional update at the computer).

Most major data base management systems can be used to create these charts. The only requirement is that the system be able to hold sufficient data to make the chart and allow for additions later on. The material can easily be fed into the computer system, sorted and printed out on demand. The list can be updated, and a new chart made, when enough changes or additional information warrant it. The chart can be tailored to suit each library's needs. These charts also make very handy aids for teachers or librarians who are

A young patron consults the North-Pulaski Subject Guide Wall Chart.

Figure 7.8: Sample Entries from Subject Guide Wall Chart

LC	Dewey	Subject
GV1111	796.8	KARATE
GV1548	791	MAGIC
M	780	MUSIC

instructing children on how to find books in the library by using the Dewey Decimal or LC systems. A simple notice should be attached to the chart which will lead patrons either to other reference tools or to the librarian if they cannot find what they want.

Results have been spectacular at North-Pulaski, the initial test site. The chart saves reference librarians an estimated one-third to one-half of all time spent normally assisting patrons with simple questions. It is a completely self-service resource, people are drawn to it naturally and it can be updated as often as the library requires. Most of the branch libraries of the Chicago Public Library now use these charts.[6]

The Software Wall Chart, illustrated in Chapter 3, can also be created using the micro and is an ideal reference tool for libraries with several hundred or more software programs. Either a word processing or specialized data base program, such as Master Catalog, can be used. Printing the material and producing a finished, laminated chart can be completed in the span of an afternoon. When patrons ask "What programs do you have?", simply refer them to the chart; it will answer most of their questions.

CONCLUSIONS

Online services are certain to play an increasingly important role in library public access efforts. The number of patrons who can access online services from home is growing, and manufacturers have begun offering modems as standard equipment with their micros. More individuals will thus be able to tap into library-produced data bases, such as the electronic bulletin board.

Services such as the library electronic bulletin board and local data bases will benefit patrons and libraries alike. As noted, patrons welcome the diversity library boards offer. Libraries can judge the needs of their patrons far better than most commercial vendors and offer services accordingly. In turn, patrons will perceive the library as an institution that can meet their needs and adapt readily to change.

Not all patrons will have access to online services from home, however, just as not all will own micros. Public access to remote online data bases, via the library, will play a vital role in bridging the gulf between the information-rich and the information-poor, thus continuing the tradition of the public library.

NOTES

1. Ward Christensen and Randy Seuss, "Hobbyist Computerized Bulletin Board," *Byte* 3 (November 1978):150.

2. "Librarian's Bulletin-Board System," *Small Computers In Libraries* 2 (October 1982): 5.

3. For a more complete account of the ABBS at the North-Pulaski Branch Library see Patrick R. Dewey, "Dear ABBS: Marketing, Maintenance, and Suggestions," *Small Computers In Libraries*, 2 (September 1982): 1.

4. Robert T. Grieves, "Short Circuiting Reference Books," *Time* 121 (June 13, 1983): 76.

5. Richard Moses, "Steam Engines in the Public Library; Or, Computers, Children and Library Services," *Emergency Librarian* 10 (January-February 1983): 14.

6. Patrick R. Dewey and Marvin Garber, "Easy to Use Microcomputer Generated Subject Guide Wall Chart," *Online* 7 (March 1983): 32.

Afterword:
The Future of Public Access Microcomputers

Although the future of public access microcomputers cannot be predicted with certainty, several observations can be made. There is no doubt that interest in public access is increasing. For example, at North-Pulaski we experienced a sharp rise in the number of inquires about our electronic bulletin board and other services in late 1983 and early 1984. However, there are a few obstacles to overcome before public access micros become a permanent aspect of library service. In addition, there are several issues to consider regarding the evolution of public access in the library.

A principal concern of anyone purchasing a microcomputer today is obsolescence, and libraries are no exception. Typical questions are: Will the equipment be outmoded before it is in place? Should we wait until things settle down a bit? Will next year's hardware last longer? Don't count on it. Things just will not settle down. No matter when you buy or what you buy, something smaller and better will come along in a very short time.

However, in the long run, obsolescence is really a superficial concern. A small investment such as a microcomputer should not be expected to last forever; three to five years is a good return on investment. I have owned the same Apple II micro for about six years and I suspect that I should be able to keep it for the next four or five years with little difficulty. Of course, it is not exactly the same machine that was originally purchased—it has been expanded and upgraded as new parts became available.

For a library considering a micro for its patrons, the important thing to remember is that time lost is service lost to the public. Viewed in this light, the benefits of owning a micro now outweigh the prospects of obsolescence.

Funding is another hurdle that libraries must overcome. In order for public access to take its place alongside other permanent library services, significant ongoing sources of funding must be found.

One positive sign is the increase in the allocation of LSCA funds for computer literacy programs in libraries. During the past two years, LSCA funds have been a significant source of funding, on a statewide or system-wide basis, for adult programs. The California State Library and Southern Adirondack Library System public access projects described in Chapter 5 are examples of this trend. The emphasis on adult education is particularly important. Large numbers of children are introduced to micros through public schools; adults who cannot buy their own machines have fewer opportunities. It is worthwhile to check with your local state library to see if such funds are or will be available in the near future.

As more and more libraries offer public access services on an ongoing basis, questions may arise as to where these services belong in the overall library structure. Some believe that, since public access involves hardware and software, it should therefore be under the jurisdiction of data processing specialists. Not so. Even though public access involves computer technology, as a public service it should be under the direct supervision and development of public service librarians. Data processing or similar staff should be available for consultation and, in some library systems, should be responsible for the installation and maintenance of the equipment. Beyond that, librarians should be responsible for any public relations, promotion, software development, management and decisions pertaining to public access. As librarians, we should see that we retain our professional prerogatives.

Finally, we must ensure that public access micros are properly integrated within the overall framework of library services. Although the microcomputer has brought with it a fundamental change in the way we look at life and the way we interact with our environment, it does not mean that we should give up all else in pursuit. Books and journals have served public needs for centuries; computers have yet to prove themselves.

While the ultimate use of the microcomputer is far from certain, its place in today's library is clear. It is a significant tool for disseminating information, and it is a powerful tool, at least for the moment, with which to promote the library, all for a reasonable investment. There is no doubt, at least in my mind, that microcomputers represent the most exciting addition to public service in recent memory.

Appendix A: Friends of the Chicago Public Library—Grant Proposal*

submitted by

Patrick R. Dewey, Unit Head
North-Pulaski Branch Library
4041 W. North Ave.
Chicago, Illinois 60639
312-235-2727

Summary of Request

This request is for a microcomputer system for the North-Pulaski Branch Library (4041 W. North Avenue) by Patrick R. Dewey, Branch Head. Such equipment would be used in the test program by the Public Access Computer Committee (PACC), the final goal of which is to establish a microcomputer network throughout the CPL branches, allowing public and staff to participate in an interconnecting system of home computers for recreational and educational uses. Guidelines shall be those established by the committee. Total amount requested is: (dollar amount omitted).

Introduction

The Public Access Computer Committee has been working for several months on a strategy for the implementation of a microcomputing network for public and staff use. This system will provide access to large numbers of computer programs of various types conveniently. The North-Pulaski Branch Library will provide an ideal setting for this test program because of the great demand by the North-Pulaski community for many of the skills for which the computer can provide instruction. The community has a large Spanish-speaking population and, in addition to English classes and GED instruction, there is a constant need and demand for remedial math, reading, and other skills. Patrick Dewey (Branch Head at North-Pulaski) has several years of personal experience with microcomputers and owns his own Apple computer system (disk drive, printer, and about 1000 computer programs which he has accumulated). He is a member of the Public Access Computer Committee.

---

*Reprinted courtesy of the Friends of the Chicago Public Library. Material is updated to reflect changes in technology and methodology that have taken place since the original grant was prepared. Because of the large fluctuations in hardware and software prices, all dollar amounts have been omitted.

Needs Assessment

The need is to test many of the assumptions and guidelines set down by PACC in its attempt to provide access to a large and hitherto untouched resource base through microcomputers to a number of different library publics, including educational, informational, and recreational software and databases. The Public Access Computer Committee has produced a list of uses for microcomputers in the library. These uses include public education (typing, foreign language, remedial skills, PLATO type instruction, etc.) and recreational (problem solving, mind challenging games, chess, etc.) and informational services. Other services are also potentially available for development such as electronic mail, and staff utilities as well as custom made software for library/survival skills for patron instruction.

Program Objectives

Specific objectives include:

- Providing a test site for the various policies and ideas worked out by PACC during the next year.

- Providing a basis for small computer club meetings (both of local formation and Special Interest Groups from the Chicago Area Computer Hobbyist Exchange—CACHE).

- Providing a site where anyone interested in microcomputers may become familiar with them.

- Providing computer instruction in the use of BASIC computer language.

- Providing a resource for staff to perform many internal tasks such as cataloging or indexing of phonodiscs or special collections (for example).

- Providing a pilot program for the use of a full disk system for use by the public and staff in a CPL branch with access to large numbers of programs.

- Providing instructional benefits in many remedial areas (math, reading) and language skills (if possible) such as Spanish. Objectives are to be met within one year of origin of project.

Methods

The entire library staff at North-Pulaski Branch shall be trained on the equipment, although the professional staff shall be directly responsible for all maintenance and oversight.

The librarians at North-Pulaski shall work closely with PACC and follow the policies worked out with the Committee.

Publicity efforts (including newsletters, etc.) shall make an effort to contact computer hobbyists in the area to solicit their ideas and perhaps solicit them to act as library volunteers. These same efforts shall also be made through CACHE.

Use of the equipment shall be by appointment.

Evaluation

The librarians at North-Pulaski Branch and the members of the Public Access Computer Committee shall be the evaluators of the project.

Records of usage by the public of the machines shall be maintained. A determination of the numbers and types of computer users at the Branch, what types of programs they use and require and how much creativity they bring to bear on the system shall be made in evaluating the system. Determining whether we are able to develop and provide a model for instructions on how to use the computer and how easily it is marketed through newsletters, etc., shall be an important staff observation.

Evaluation and identification of problems connected with such a complex system in a public place shall be a top priority so that such problems can be avoided in the future in any expansion of the system. For example, experience with the rather limited PET computers at several branches and experience with Apple home computers by certain committee members shall be taken into account when establishing this pilot system.

Future Funding

Funding to continue or to enlarge this pilot program might come from a number of sources. The firms which manufacture microcomputers may establish grants of equipment or funding if the library works out a sufficiently convincing plan of operation (for example, Apple Computer has established a foundation for various types of computer grants). Software might possibly be purchased by the library out of budgeted funds. Large numbers of programs are already available at little or no cost through computer clubs.

It should be of considerable interest that the average number of programs available to PET users at branches is less than 100 extremely simple programs while we are here talking about hundreds (with a potential for thousands) of very complex and advanced (as well as beginner's) programs available to users.

Budget Items

(All dollar amounts have been omitted.)

Apple Computer with 64K memory and two disk drives

Apple Computer with 64K memory and one disk drive

Two nine-inch GMC Monitors

Two service contracts

D.C. Hayes Micromodem (this device allows the computer to link up with online services via the telephone system)

People's Message System (PMS) bulletin board software system

Prism Printer with controller card

Software (various kinds listed)

Expendable supplies, drive head cleaners, diskettes, paper, printer ribbons

Endorsements

Letters of support from the library Data Processing Department and the head of neighborhood services are attached.

Appendix B: Manufacturers of Microcomputers Used in Public Access Programs

Apple Computer, Inc.
20525 Mariani Ave.
Cupertino, CA 95014

Atari Inc.
1312 Crossman
Box 3427
Sunnyvale, CA 94088-3427

Commodore Business Machines, Inc.
1200 Wilson Dr.
West Chester, PA 19380

IBM Corp.
Box 1325
Boca Raton, FL 33432

Radio Shack (division of Tandy Corp.)
1800 One Tandy Center
Forth Worth, TX 76102

Texas Instruments, Inc.*
Box 53
Lubbock, TX 79408

Timex Computer Corp.
Box 2655
Waterbury, CT 06725

---

*In 1983, Texas Instruments discontinued the production of its home computer; nevertheless it intends to support existing machines.

Appendix C: Selected Software Companies

American Software Publishing Co.
Box 57221
Washington, DC 20037

Appleware Inc.
6400 Hayes St.
Hollywood, FL 33024

Borg-Warner Educational Systems
600 W. University Dr.
Arlington Heights, IL 60004

Calico
Box 15916
St. Louis, MO 63114

Cambridge Development Laboratory
30 Pleasant St.
Watertown, MA 02172

Charles W. Clark Co., Inc.
168 Express Dr. S.
Brentwood, NY 11717

COMPress
Box 102
Wentworth, NH 03282

Computer Systems Research, Inc.
40 Darling Dr.
Avon Park S.
Avon, CT 06001

Compuware
15 Center Rd.
Randolph, NJ 07869

Conduit
Box 388
Iowa City, IA 52244

Continental Software
11223 S. Hindry Ave.
Los Angeles, CA 90045

Control Data Publishing Co. (PLATO)
Box 261127
San Diego, CA 92126

Dynacomp, Inc.
1427 Monroe Ave.
Rochester, NY 14618

Educational Activities, Inc.
Box 392
Freeport, NY 11520

Educational Courseware
3 Nappa Lane
Westport, CT 06880

Edutek Corp.
415 Cambridge 14
Palo Alto, CA 94306

Edu-Ware Services, Inc.
Box 22222
Agoura, CA 91301

Fisher Scientific Co.
Educational Materials Division
4901 W. LeMoyne St.
Chicago, IL 60651

Follett Library Book Co.
4506 Northwest Highway
Crystal Lake, IL 60014

GAF Software
127 Mount Spring Rd.
Tolland, CT 06084

Hayden Book Co., Inc.
50 Essex St.
Rochelle Park, NJ 07662

Houghton Mifflin Co.
One Beacon St.
Boston, MA 02108

Ingram Book Co.
347 Reedwood Dr.
Box 17266
Nashville, TN 37217

Instant Software, Inc.
Route 101 and Elm St.
Peterborough, NH 03458

K-12 MicroMedia Inc.
172 Broadway
Woodcliff Lake, NJ 07675

The Learning Co.
545 Middlefield Rd.
Suite 170
Menlo Park, CA 94025

Micro Learningware
Highway 66 S.
Box 307
Mankato, MN 56001

Micro Power and Light Co.
12820 Hillcrest Rd.
Dallas, TX 75230

Microlab
2310 Skokie Valley Rd.
Highland Park, IL 60035

Microphys Programs
1737 W. 2nd St.
Brooklyn, NY 11223

MicroPro International Corp.
33 San Pablo Ave.
San Rafael, CA 94903

Microsoft Corp.
10700 Northup Way
Bellevue, WA 98004

Midwest Visual Equipment Co.
6500 N. Hamlin Ave.
Chicago, IL 60645

Milliken Publishing Co.
1100 Research Blvd.
St. Louis, MO 63132

Minnesota Educational Computing
   Consortium (MECC)
2520 Broadway Dr.
St. Paul, MN 55113

Muse Software
347 N. Charles St.
Baltimore, MD 21201

Ombudsman Educational Services, Inc.
1585 N. Milwaukee Ave.
Libertyville, IL 60048

Opportunities for Learning, Inc.
8950 Luline Ave.
Chatsworth, CA 91311

PDQ Software
11 Eider Court
Greenwich, CT 06830

Program Design, Inc.
95 E. Putnam Ave.
Greenwich, CT 06830

Programs for Learning, Inc.
Box 954
53 Bank St.
New Milford, CT 06776

Quality Educational Designs
Box 12486
Portland, OR 97212

Queue, Inc.
5 Chapel Hill Dr.
Fairfield, CT 06432

Rainbow Computing Inc.
19517 Business Center Dr.
Northridge, CA 91324

Random House School Division
400 Hahn Rd.
Westminster, MD 21157

Right On Programs
Box 977
Huntington, NY 11743

Scarborough Systems
25 N. Broadway
Tarrytown, NY 10591

Scholastic, Inc.
730 Broadway
New York, NY 10003

Science Research Associates, Inc.
155 N. Wacker Dr.
Chicago, IL 60606

Sierra On-Line, Inc.
Sierra On-Line Building
Coarsegold, CA 93614

Sirius Software, Inc.
10364 Rockingham Dr.
Sacramento, CA 95827

Sir-Tech Software, Inc.
6 Main St.
Ogdensburg, NY 13669

Society for Visual Education
1345 Diversey Pkwy.
Chicago, IL 60614

Softswap
San Mateo County Office of Education
333 Main St.
Redwood City, CA 94063

Software Discount House
Nolan Information Management
   Services
21203-A Hawthorne Blvd.
Suite 5323
Torrance, CA 90509

Sorcim Corp.
2310 Lundy Ave.
San Jose, CA 95131

Spinnaker Software
215 First St.
Cambridge, MA 02142

SubLogic Corp.
713 Edgebrook Dr.
Champaign, IL 61820

The 3 R's
815 Broadway
Rockford, IL 61108

TIES
1925 W. County Rd. B2
St. Paul, MN 55113

VisiCorp.
2895 Zanker Rd.
San Jose, CA 91534

Appendix D: Selected Coinop Companies

The Computer Mart of New Hampshire, Inc.
170 Main St.
Nashua, NH 03060

Computer Solutions
2716 Erie Blvd.
Syracuse, NY 13224

Gaylord Bros., Inc.
Box 4901
Syracuse, NY 13221

Maxwell Library Systems at Boston Copico
1400K Providence Highway
Norwood, MA 02062

Micro Timesharing Co.
470 Belmont Dr.
Box 4658
Salinas, CA 93912

Tava Corp.
16861 Armstrong Ave.
Irvine, CA 92714

Appendix E: Microcomputer Newsletters and Journals

Byte
McGraw-Hill Inc.
70 Main St.
Peterborough, NH 03458

Classroom Computer Learning
Pitman Learning, Inc.
6 Davis Dr.
Belmont, CA 94002

Computer Shopper
Patch Publishing, Inc.
Box F
407 S. Washington Ave.
Titusville, FL 32780

Computers and the Media Center (CMC News)
Jim Deacon
515 Oak St. N
Cannon Falls, MN 55009

ComputerTown Newsbulletin
People's Computer Co.
Box E
Menlo Park, CA 94025

The Computing Teacher
International Council for Computers in Education
1787 Agate St.

University of Oregon
Eugene, OR 97403

CP/M Review
Review Publications
2711 76th Ave., SE
Mercer Island, WA 98040

Creative Computing
Ziff-Davis Publishing
One Park Ave.
New York, NY 10016

Easy Home Computer
Pumpkin Press
350 Fifth Ave.
Suite 6204
New York, NY 10118

Educational Computer
Dundee Maples
3199 de la Cruz
Santa Clara, CA 95050

ETC: Educational Technology and Communication
Far West Laboratory for Educational Research and Development
1855 Folsom St.
San Francisco, CA 94103

Hot Off the Computer
Westchester Library System
8 Westchester Plaza
Elmsford, NY 10523

Library HI TECH
Pierian Press, Inc.
Box 1808
Ann Arbor, MI 48106

Link-Up
On-Line Communications
3938 Meadowbrook Rd.
Minneapolis, MN 55426

Modem Notes
Katherine Ackerman
Box 408472
Chicago, IL 60640

PC World
PC World Communications, Inc.
555 De Haro St.
San Francisco, CA 94107

Personal Computing
Hayden Publishing Co., Inc.
50 Essex St.
Rochelle Park, NJ 07662

Personal Software
Hayden Publishing Co., Inc.
50 Essex St.
Rochelle Park, NJ 07662

Popular Computing
McGraw-Hill Inc.
70 Main St.
Peterborough, NH 03458

School Library Media Quarterly
American Library Association
50 E. Huron St.
Chicago, IL 60611

Small Computers in Libraries
University of Arizona
Graduate Library School
1515 E. First
Tucson, AZ 85719

Softalk
Softalk Publishing, Inc.
11160 McCormick
Box 60
North Hollywood, CA 91603

Software Review
Meckler Publishing
520 Riverside Ave.
Westport, CT 06880

Teaching and Computers
Scholastic Inc.
730 Broadway
New York, NY 10003

Appendix F: Bulletin Board Software Sources

ABBS 4.0
Software Sorcery
7927 Jones Branch Dr.
Suite 400
McLean, VA 22102
Apple II, $64.95

ACCESS
Information Intelligence, Inc.
Box 31098
Phoenix, AZ 85046
Apple II, $750

AMIS
(public domain)
GRAFex Co.
Box 1558
Cupertino, CA 95015
Atari 800, $10

Bullet-80
Computer Services of Danbury
1 Franklin St.
Box 993
Danbury, CT 06810
TRS-80 I, $13; TRS-80 III, $150

Bulletin Board System
Miracle Computing
313 Clayton Court
Lawrence, KS 66044
IBM, $99

CBBS
Randy Suess, CBBS
5219 W. Warwick
Chicago, IL 60641
CP/M, $50

CommuniTree
Network, Inc.
Box 2246
Dept. TC
Berkeley, CA 94702
Apple II, $250

CP/M
CP/M Users Group
1651 Third Ave.
New York, NY 10028
Public domain

Forum-80
Small Business Systems Group
6 Carlisle Rd.
Westford, MA 01866
TRS-80 I and III, $350

HOSTCOMM
N.F. Systems Ltd.
Box 76363
Atlanta, GA 30358
IBM, $170

MOUSE-NET
Lance Micklus, Inc.
217 S. Union St.
Burlington, VT 05401
TRS-80 I and III, $299

Net-Works
Nick Naimo
4877 Martin Rd.
Newburgh, IN 47630
Apple II, $89.95

People's Message System (PMS)
Datel Systems, Inc.
8624 Cuyamaca St.
Suite D
Santee, CA 92071
Apple II, $300

Glossary

Applications software: A program designed to solve a specific problem or perform a certain task for the user.

BASIC: Beginner's All-purpose Symbolic Instruction Code. A simple, high-level, computer language.

Bit: Binary Digit. The smallest unit of computer information (a one or a zero).

Buffer: A storage area, also called a "spooler." Buffers are usually reserved storage locations in main memory or peripheral devices.

Byte: A group of bits (usually eight) that act as a unit (e.g., a character, numeral, etc.). A computer's memory is measured in bytes.

Chip: A silicon wafer or integrated circuit (IC) package. A microprocessor chip has thousands of electrical circuits engraved on it through which it communicates with the rest of the computer system.

COBOL: Common Business-Oriented Language. A high-level (English-like) language widely used in business applications software.

CAI: Computer Assisted Instruction. Programs providing online direct interactive instruction, testing and prescription.

CP/M: Control Program for Microcomputers. A trade name of Digital Research, Inc. for an operating system used on many 8-bit microcomputers.

CPU: Central Processing Unit. The "brain" of the computer, the part that controls the interpretation and execution of machine instructions. Microcomputers use microprocessor chips for the CPU.

CRT: Cathode Ray Tube. A computer terminal for data display with a television-like screen. Also called a monitor.

Data Base: A collection of data that are stored electronically and can be retrieved and manipulated in a number of ways.

DBMS: Data Base Management System. A software system that manages the storage, access, updating and maintenance of a data base.

Debug: To find the errors in a program and to correct them.

Disk drive: The mechanism used for mass random access storage of data including both the storage medium (disks) and the machinery to spin it at a controlled speed.

Disk operating system (DOS): Used as a generic term by vendors to indicate an operating system capable of handling mass memory hard or floppy disk storage.

Disk storage: A mass storage medium incorporating one or more magnetic disks that may be grouped into units called disk packs or cartridges if the disk is hard, or thin flexible plastic cases for floppy diskettes.

Download: To transfer data from a larger computer, system or file to a smaller one.

Downtime: The time during which a computer system or one of its parts is not functioning.

Firmware: Software or data stored in a fixed way or built into a ROM system, as opposed to disks or tapes that are entered into RAM.

Hard copy: A printed copy of machine output, as opposed to soft copy such as voice output or copy on a screen.

Hardware: All of the tangible components of the computer system, including the computer, diskettes, drive, keyboard, etc. To be distinguished from software, or instructions.

Input: The process of entering data into the computer usually by typing at the keyboard.

Joystick: A small lever used mostly for controlling play in arcade games.

Keyboard: The device used for typing data or instructions into the micro.

LOGO: A computer language specially designed for teaching programming to young children.

Machine language: A programming language that is understood directly by the machine, requiring no translation.

Mainframe: A full-sized computer (usually costing more than $1 million), the memory of which is usually measured in megabytes (millions of bytes). These large computers are typically used by municipalities, academic institutions and other large organizations.

Memory: The storage of a computer. Internal memory stores both programs that are being executed and data that are being processed. The amount of internal memory determines the complexity of programs that can be used and may affect how fast the programs can be run.

Microcomputer: A computer that uses a microprocessor chip as its CPU, hence the term, "computer on a chip."

Minicomputer: A mid-range computer (between a micro and a mainframe) that has a central processing unit, at least one input-output device and a primary storage capacity of at least 64,000 characters.

Modem: *Mo*dulator/*dem*odulator. A device that translates digital computer signals into analog telephone signals, making computer signals compatible with communications facilities. The speed at which modems operate is expressed in baud, measured in bits per second.

Operating system: Software that controls the overall operations of a computer, handling routine data transfer operations among computer components and peripheral devices.

Output: The communication of results to the user after the computer has finished its processing. Output can be through the monitor (screen), printer or voice synthesizer.

PASCAL: A high-level language originally intended to teach programming as a systematic discipline and to do systems-level programming. This language is now in wider use and is occasionally proposed as a replacement for BASIC as a beginner's language.

Peripherals: The other hardware components of a computer system besides the CPU. Peripherals include the printer, disk drive, console, terminal, etc. If any of these are removed from the system, the computer will still be able to function, even if less efficiently.

Program: A set of instructions that tells the computer what to do.

RAM: Random Access Memory. Memory into which applications programs are read and data are manipulated. RAM changes each time programs or data are loaded or altered in some way. RAM memory is lost whenever the power is turned off.

ROM: Read Only Memory. Memory that is permanently stored in the computer's memory chips. It can be accessed but not altered by the user and is always readily available, even after a power interruption.

Software: A set of programs, procedures and documentation concerned with the operation of a computer system. There are two types: systems software and applications software.

Systems software: Programs that control the internal workings of the computer. The operating system is considered part of systems software.

Upload: To transfer data from a smaller computer, system or file to a larger one.

Selected Bibliography

CHILDREN AND COMPUTERS

Ball, Marion J., and Charp, Sylvia. *Be a Computer Literate*. Morris Plains, NJ: Creative Computing Press, 1977.

Cohen, Theodore J., and Bray, Jacqueline H. *Melissa and John and The Magic Machine*. Peterborough, NH: Byte Publications, 1978. (Coloring book).

Court, Rosemary. *Sam's System, A Guide to Computers*. Great Britain: Children's Press, 1983.

D'Ignazio, Fred. *The Star Wars Question & Answer Book About Computers*. New York: Random House, 1983.

Larsen, Sally Greenwood. *Computers For Kids*. Morris Plains, NJ: Creative Computing Press, 1981. (Available for the Apple, Atari and TRS-80).

Lipscomb, Susan Drake, and Zuanich, Margaret Ann. *Basic Fun: Computer Games, Puzzles, and Problems Children Can Write*. New York: Avon Books, 1982.

Lipson, Shelly. *It's Basic: The ABC's of Computer Programming*. New York: Holt, Rinehart & Winston, 1982.

Rice, Jean. *My Friend-The Computer*. Minneapolis, MN: TS Denison & Co., 1981.

FUND RAISING

Carry, Emmett. *Grants for the Smaller Library: Sources of Funding and Proposal Writing Techniques for the Small and Medium-Sized Library*. Littleton, CO: Libraries Unlimited, 1981.

Engbert, Robert. "Fund-Raising for Microcomputers." *Educational Computer* 2 (July/August 1982): 21.

Grasty, William, and Sheinkopf, Kenneth G. *Successful Fund Raising: A Handbook of Proven Strategies and Techniques*. New York: The Scribner Book Cos., 1982.

Kenton, Pattie, and Ernst, Mary. "Finding Funds for Microcomputers." *Instructional Innovator* 26 (September 1981): 32.

Neumann, Robert. "How to Raise Money in Your Community." *Electronic Learning* 2 (September 1982): 43.

Spiva, Ulysses V. *How to Get A Grant for Your Own Special Project.* Bloomington, IN: T.I.S., Inc., 1980.

Thomas, James L. "Appendix III: Funding Sources for Microcomputers." In *Microcomputers In the Schools*, p. 137. Phoenix, AZ: Oryx Press, 1981.

HARDWARE

AASL Committee for Standardization of Access to Library Media Resources. "Microcomputer Software and Hardware—An Annotated Source List." *School Library Media Quarterly* (Winter 1984): 107.

Blair, John C. Jr. "Micro Magic." *Online* 6 (May 1982): 69.

Crosby, Mark L. "Singin' the Disk I/O Blues." *Apple Orchard* 2 (Winter 1981/82): 63.

Glossbrenner, Alred. *The Complete Handbook of Personal Computer Communications.* New York: St. Martin's Press, 1983.

Health Hazards of CRTs. Chico, CA: Ryan Research International, 1983.

McClain, Larry. "Servicing Your System: Be Prepared." *Personal Computing* 6 (September 1982): 50.

Meilach, Dona Z. *Before You Buy a Computer.* New York: Crown Publishers, 1983.

Microcomputer Hardware and Software in the El-Hi Market, 1983-87. White Plains, NY: Knowledge Industry Publications, Inc., 1983.

Rorvig, Mark E. *Microcomputers and Libraries: A Guide to Technology, Products and Applications.* White Plains, NY: Knowledge Industry Publications, Inc., 1981.

Sullivan, Roll A. *Microcomputer Selection and Criteria: Educator's Edition.* Washington, DC: American Microcomputer Association, 1981.

Townsend, Carl. *How to Get Started With CP/M.* Beaverton, OR: Dilithium Press, 1981.

Walsh, Myles E. *Understanding Computers: What Managers and Users Need to Know.* New York: John Wiley & Sons, 1981.

Woods, Lawrence A., and Pope, Nolan F. *The Librarian's Guide to Microcomputer Technology and Applications.* White Plains, NY: Knowledge Industry Publications, Inc., 1983.

Zaks, Rodnay. *DON'T! (or How to Care for Your Computer).* Berkeley, CA: Sybex, 1981.

INTRODUCTION TO COMPUTERS

Corbett, Scott. *Home Computers, A Simple and Informative Guide.* Boston, MA: Little, Brown & Co., 1980.

Costa, Betty, and Costa, Marie. *Micro Handbook for Small Libraries and Media Centers.* Littletown, CO: Libraries Unlimited, 1983.

Deken, Joseph. *The Electronic Cottage.* New York: Bantam Books, 1981.

Frederick, Franz. *Guide to Microcomputers.* Washington, DC: Association for Educational Communications and Technology, 1980.

Galanter, Eugene. *Kids and Computers, The Parents' Microcomputer Handbook.* New York: Perigee Books, 1983.

Lieff, Jonathan D. *How to Buy a Personal Computer Without Anxiety.* New York: Harper & Row Publishers, 1982.

Ouverson, Marlin. *Computer Anatomy for Beginners.* Reston, VA: Reston Publishing, 1982.

Prenis, John. *Running Press Glossary of Computer Terms.* Philadelphia, PA: Running Press, 1977.

Sippl, Charles J., and Mayer, JoAnne Coffman. *The Essential Computer Dictionary and Speller.* Englewood Cliffs, NJ: Prentice-Hall, 1980.

Spencer, Donald D. *Computer Dictionary for Everyone.* New York: The Scribner Book Cos., 1979.

Townsend, Carl. *How to Get Started With CP/M.* Beaverton, OR: Dilithium Press, 1981.

Walton, Robert A. *Microcomputers: A Planning and Implementation Guide for Librarians and Information Professionals.* Phoenix, AZ: Oryx Press, 1983.

Willis, Jerry, and Miller, Merl. *Computers for Everybody.* Beaverton, OR: Dilithium Press, 1981.

PUBLIC ACCESS PROJECTS

Adiletta, William F. *The Chicago Public Library: Public Access Computer Report* (Document #A1301381). June 1981.

"Chicago, Illinois has Thriving Computer Center." *Library Journal* 107 (April 1, 1982): 674.

Cohen, Dorren. "Public Access Micros: ComputerTown USA!" *Access* 2 (October 1982): 5

Computer Literacy Project. Report available from Tacoma Public Library, 1102 Tacoma Ave. S., Tacoma, WA 98402.

Dewey, Patrick R. "A Microcomputer for Staff and Public Use." *Illinois Libraries* 64 (September 1982): 880.

———. "Problems in the Personal Computer Center." *Small Computers In Libraries* 2 (April 1982): 1.

———. "The Personal Computer Center at the North-Pulaski Library." *Educational Computer* 3 (March/April 1983): 28.

Duncan, Carol S. "Compulit: Computer Literacy for Tacoma." *Library Journal* (January 1984): 52-53.

Edmonds, Leslie. "Taming Technology: Planning for Patron Use of Microcomputers in the Public Library." *Top of the News* 39 (Spring 1983): 247.

Fabian, William M. "An Apple for the Librarian: Microcomputers and Instruction." *Show-Me Libraries* 33 (March 1982): 5.

Fowler, Bonnie S., and Smith, Duncan. "Microcomputers for the Public In the Public Library." *Information Technology and Libraries* 2 (March 1983): 46.

Hirshberg, Peter. "Compu-Tots and Other Joys of Museum Life." *Instructional Innovator* 26 (September 1981): 29.

Hunter, Beverly. "Computer Literacy." Paper presented at the Patterns Conference on Computer Literacy, p. 3, April 27-28, 1981, in Rochester, NY.

Kusack, James, and Bowers, John S. "Public Microcomputers In Public Libraries." *Library Journal* 107 (November 15, 1982): 2137.

Loop, Liza. "Upper Arlington ComputerTown Report." *ComputerTown News Bulletin* 4 (May/June 1983): 1.

Loop, Liza; Anton, Julie; and Zamora, Ramon. *ComputerTown: A Do-It-Yourself Community Computer Project.* Menlo Park, CA: People's Computer Co., 1982.

Moses, Richard. "Steam Engines in the Public Library; Or, Computers, Children and Library Services." *Emergency Librarian* 10 (January/February 1983): 14.

Piele, Linda J. "Circulating Microcomputer Software." *Public Access: Microcomputers In Libraries* 2 (October 1982): 7.

Roberts, Ken. "The Oakville Public Library's Computer Program For Young People: A Critique." *Emergency Librarian* 10 (January/February 1983): 16.

Romans, Anne F., and Ransom, Stanley A. "An Apple a Day: Microcomputers in the Public Library." *American Libraries* 11 (December 1980): 691.

Shair, Harold M. "Coin-in-the-Slot Computing at a Public Library." *Creative Computing* 3 (May/June 1977): 36.

"Two N.Y. Libraries Provide Computer Education." *Library Journal* 107 (June 1, 1982): 1041.

Zamora, Ramon. "ComputerTown, USA! Using Personal Computers in the Public Library." *School Library Journal* 27 (April 1981): 28.

SOFTWARE

Brown, Marijke. "Library Skills." *RQ* 22 (Summer 1983): 414.

Christensen, Jane. *Word Processing Simplified and Self-Taught.* New York: Arco Publishing, 1983.

Christie, Linda Gail. "How to Evaluate Documentation Manuals." *Interface Age* 7 (August 1982): 61.

Cole, Phyllis. "Educational Software." *People's Computers* 6 (May/June 1978): 58.

Educational Software Directory: A Subject Guide to Microcomputer Software. Compiled by Marilyn J. Chartrand and Constance D. Williams. Littleton, CO: Libraries Unlimited, 1982.

Emard, Jean-Paul. "Software Hang-ups and Glitches: Problems to be Faced and Overcome." *Online* 7 (January 1983): 18.

"Evaluation Criteria for Microcomputer Software." *Booklist* 78 (October 1, 1981): 243.

Frenzel, Louis E. Jr. "Where to Buy Your Software." *Interface Age* 7 (April 1982): 122.

Gordon, Anita, and Zinn, Karl. "Microcomputer Software Considerations." *School Library Journal* (August 1982): 25.

Heck, William P.; Johnson, Jerry; and Kansky, R.J. *Guidelines for Evaluating Instructional Materials*. Reston, VA: National Council of Teachers of Mathematics, 1981.

Henderson, Thomas B.; Cobb, Douglass Ford; and Cobb, Gena Berg. *Spreadsheet Software From VisiCalc to 1-2-3.* Indianapolis, IN: Que Corp., 1983.

Hilgenfeld, R. "Checking Out Software." *The Computing Teacher* 9 (November 1981): 24.

Judd, Dorothy H., and Judd, Robert C., "Evaluation of Instructional Programs for Microcomputers." *Educational Computer* 2 (March/April 1982): 16.

Lathrop, Ann. "Building the Software Collection." *Educational Computer* 1 (November/December 1981):23.

———. "Softswap Educational Software Exchange—Will Your Group Donate the Next Disk?" *The Computing Teacher* 9 (May 1982): 48.

———. "Terrible Ten: Ten Reasons for Rejecting Software." *Educational Computer,* (September/October 1982).

Mason, Robert M. "Searching for Software: Finding and Buying the 'Right Stuff'." *Library Journal* 107 (April 15, 1983): 801.

McWilliams, Peter. *The Word Processing Book.* Los Angeles, CA: Prelude Press, 1982.

Meilach, Dona Z. "Spelling Programs: The Proof's in the Printing." *Interface Age* 7 (May 1982): 74.

Price, Robert. "Selecting Free and Inexpensive Computer Software." *Educational Computer* 2 (May/June 1982): 24.

"Quality Software: How to Know When You've Found It!" *Electronic Learning* 1 (November/December 1981): 33.

Strackbein, Ray, and Strackbein, Dorothy Bowlby. *Computers and Data Processing Simplified and Self-Taught.* New York: Arco Publishing, 1983.

Watt, Daniel. "Close Encounters With Software." *Popular Computing* (August 1982): 36.

Watt, Molly. "Making a Case for Software Evaluation." *The Computing Teacher* 9 (May 1982): 20.

Woolls, Blanche E., and Loertscher, David V. "Some Sure-Fire Microcomputer Programs." *School Library Journal* (August 1982): 22.

TELECOMMUNICATIONS AND ONLINE SERVICES

Archibald, Dale. "What Is and What's to Come in Telecommunications, Part I." *Softalk* 3 (January 1983): 186.

———. "What Is and What's to Come in Telecommunications, Part II." *Softalk* 3 (March 1983): 99.

———. "What Is and What's to Come in Telecommunications, Part III." *Softalk* 3 (June 1983): 172.

Christensen, Ward, and Seuss, Randy. "Hobbyist Computerized Bulletin Board." *Byte* 3 (November 1978): 150.

Coffey, Michael. "The Better Bulletin Board System." *Creative Computing* 8 (December 1982): 20.

Dewey, Patrick R. "Dear ABBS: Marketing, Maintenance, and Suggestions." *Small Computers In Libraries* 2 (September 1982): 1.

Dewey, Patrick R., and Garber, Marvin. "Easy to Use Microcomputer Generated Subject Guide Wall Chart." *Online* 7 (March 1983): 32.

Edelhart, Mike, and Davies, Owen, eds. *Omni Online Data Base Directory.* New York: Macmillan Publishing, 1983

Grieves, Robert T. "Short Circuiting Reference Books." *Time* 121 (June 13, 1983): 76.

"Librarian's Bulletin-Board System." *Small Computers In Libraries* 2 (October 1982): 5.

Lundell, Allan. "Conference Tree Branches Out." *Infoworld* 3 (May 25, 1981): 3.

The Source User's Manual. McLean, VA: Source Telecomputing Corp., 1981.

"Sources of Bulletin Board Software." *Personal Computing* 7 (July 1983): 13.

Tenopir, Carol. "Dialog's Knowledge Index and BRS/After Dark: Database Searching on Personal Computers." *Library Journal* 108 (March 1, 1983): 471.

The, Lee. "Data Communications: A Buyer's Guide to Modems and Software." *Personal Computing* 7 (March 1983): 96.

Vaughn, Craig W. "Bulletin-Board Evolution Enhances Communication." *InfoWorld* 3 (May 25, 1981): 33.

Wilburn, Gene and Wilburn, Marion. "Microcomputer-based Bulletin Board System: Free Videotext and Electronic Message Services." In *Microcomputers For Libraries: How Useful Are They?*, edited by Jane Beaumont and Donald Kruger. Ottowa: Canadian Library Association, 1983.

Index

ABI/Inform, 117
Academic American Encyclopedia, 117
Activities for Computer Classes, 95
The Addison-Wesley Book of Apple Computer Software, 22
The Addison-Wesley Book of Atari Computer Software, 23
The Addison-Wesley Book of IBM Computer Software, 25
Alice and Hamilton Fish Library, 64, 67
American Library Association (ALA), 41
American Software Publishing Co., 44
Anchor Pad International, 52
Apple Computer, 13, 21-22, 34, 47, 48, 49, 50, 52, 67, 76
   Apple II, 21, 44, 47, 73, 79, 80, 85, 123
   Apple IIe, 20, 21, 27, 72, 73, 74, 75, 79, 81, 85
   Apple II+, 71, 77, 79, 84
   Apple III, 20, 21
   Macintosh, 20, 21
Apple Library Users Groups (ALUG), 90
Applefreeloader: Guide to Public Domain Software for Apple Computers, 44
Appleware Inc., 44
Applications Software Sourcebook, 26
Arlington Heights Memorial Library, 40
ASCII Express, 110
Atari Inc., 22-23, 44, 47, 48, 49, 50
   Atari 400, 22-23, 74, 75
   Atari 800, 22-23
   Atari 600XL, 23
   Atari 800XL, 23
Atariwriter, 47

A Bay Area Guide to Computer Stores, 74
Bell & Howell, 119
Bibliographic Retrieval Services (BRS), 42, 115. See also BRS After Dark
Biosis Previews, 117
Bluebook for the Apple Computer, 22
Bluebook for the Atari Computer, 23
Bluebook for the IBM Computer, 25
Booklist, 41
Books in Print, 117
BRS After Dark, 42, 103, 115, 116-117
A Buyer's Guide to the Right Computer, 74
Byte, 41

Calico, 32, 47
California State Library, 13, 70, 84, 124
Callaghan, Linda, 59
CA Search, 117
Castle Wolfenstein, 85
Chicago Public Library, 70-71, 119
Classic Library Programs, 32, 47
Classroom Computer Learning, 41
Coinop companies, 4, 26-27
Commodore Business Machines, 23-24
   CBM 8032, 24, 44, 50
   CBM 8096, 50
   Commodore PET, 20, 24, 44, 47, 49, 70, 71, 73, 74
   Commodore 64, 19, 23, 47, 48, 73, 74
   Commodore SuperPET, 24
   Commodore VIC 20, 20, 23, 44, 50, 75, 80
Commodore Educational Software Package, 44
The Complete Handbook of Personal Computer Communications, 111

CompuRead 3.0, 47
CompuServe, 4, 5, 75, 115, 116, 117
CompuSpell, 47
CompuVend, 26
Computer Mart of New Hampshire, 27
Computer Shopper, 89
Computer Systems Research, Inc., 49
ComputerTown News Bulletin, 74
ComputerTown USA!, 3, 70, 74-75
Computer-Using Educators, 44
Compuware, 48
Continental Software, 48
Control Data Publishing Co., 49
Coordinated Occupational Information Network (COIN), 119
CP/M User's Group, 44
Cranston Manor, 49, 79
Creative Computing, 41

The Dark Crystal, 49
The Data Factory, 33, 45, 47, 119
Data Pro Directory of Small Computers, 21, 41
Data Pro Research Corp., 41
Dialog Information Services, 41, 115. *See also* Knowledge Index
Digest of Software Reviews, 41
Directory of Microcomputer Software, 41
Douglass Branch Library, 73
Dow Jones News/Retrieval Service, 115, 117
Downers Grove Public Library, 75
DynaComp, 50

Educational Computer, 41
Edu-Ware Services, Inc., 47
Ernie's Quiz, 85
Electronic bulletin board system (BBS), 3
  defined, 104
  downloading from, 110
  history of, 103-104
  maintenance of, 112-114
  operation of, 105-109
  selecting, 111-112
English as a Second Language (ESL), 32, 97

Facemaker, 47
FCM, 33, 47
Fisher Scientific Co., 44
Folklife Terminal Club, 44
Forsyth County Public Library, 5
Frankfort Public Library, 76-77

Gamemaster, 72, 95
General Education Development (GED), 32, 97
Gertrude's Puzzles, 48
Gertrude's Secrets, 48
Grace A. Dow Memorial Library, 64
Groton Public Library, 97
Guidelines for Cataloging Microcomputer Software, 45

Harvard Business Review Online, 117
Haunted House, 48
Hayden Book Co., 49
Hewlett-Packard, 75
Home Accountant, 48
Hunter, Beverly, 4
Hurkle, 48

IBM Corp., 24-25, 34
  IBM PC, 20, 24, 47, 48, 49, 50, 52, 75
  IBM PCjr, 20, 24-25
  IBM PC XT, 24
Infocom Software, 50
INFOPORT, 103-104
International Software Directory, 42

Kernersville Branch Library, 90
Knowledge Index, 41, 42, 115, 116-117
Know Your Apple, 48
Know Your Apple IIe, 48

The Learning Co., 48
Library Microcomputer Users, 90
Library Services and Construction Act (LSCA), 13, 70, 73, 84, 124
Library Skills, 32
Lincoln Library, 93
Liverpool Public Library, 77-78
Local data bases, 119-121
LOGO, 48, 79, 85

Magic Spells, 48
Management of Small Computers, 41
A Manual of AACR2 Examples for Microcomputer Software and Video Games, 45
Master Catalog, 45, 121
Master Type: The Typing Instruction Game, 48
Maxwell Library Systems at Boston Copico, 27
Maywood Public Library, 79
MCI, Inc., 117

MEDLINE, 117
Menlo Park Public Library, 34, 74-75
Microcomputer
    abuse, 64-65
    care of, 54
    manufacturers, 21-26, 28
    security, 52
    selecting for public access, 15-21
    technology, 7-12
        See also Public access, Software
Microcomputer Index, 41, 117
Microcomputer Information Services, 41
Microcomputer Questions and Answers, 74
Microcomputer Users Group for Libraries in North Carolina (MUGLNC), 90
Microlab, 47
MicroPro International Corp., 50
MicroSIFT, 42
Micro-Software Services, Inc., 42
Micro Timesharing, 27
Microsoft Corp., 50
Microzine, 48
Mid-Hudson Library System, 67
Midwest Visual Equipment Co., 52
Minnesota Educational Computing Consortium (MECC), 36, 44, 48, 49, 95
Mission Asteroid, 49
Modems, 11, 105
Muse Software, 48, 50
Mystery House, 48-49

National Newspaper Index (NNI), 117
National Science Foundation, 74
National Technical Information Service (NTIS), 117
Native American Information and Referral Center, 119
Net-Works, 112
The New Step by Step, 49
News & Review, 90
North Austin Branch Library, 94
North Central Regional Library, 64
North-Pulaski Branch Library, 1, 4, 30, 48, 58, 64, 71-72, 92, 95, 97, 101, 104-105, 106, 107, 108, 110, 111, 113, 114, 119, 121, 123
Northwest Regional Education Laboratory, 42

Oakville Public Library, 93-94, 118
Odell Lake, 49
Odell Woods, 49

Online Inc., 42
Online Micro-software Guide and Directory, 42
Oregon Trail, 49
Osborne Computer, 75

Painter Power, 85
PA Micro, 90
Parmlee Billings Library, 95
P.D.Q. Software, 49
People's Computer Co. See ComputerTown USA!
People's Message System (PMS), 104, 112
Perfect Writer, 85
Personal Computing, 41
Pie Writer (Pie 2.2), 34, 49
PLATO, 49
Popular Computing, 64
Portsmouth Public Library, 80
Preschool I.Q. Builder, 35, 49
Primer, 49
Princess and the Wizard, 48-49
Princeton High School Library, 117
Program Design Inc., 49
PsychINFO, 117
Public access
    activities, 92-97
    areas of service, 5-6
    clubs, 87-90
    costs, 62-63
    defined, 3
    evaluating service, 65
    examples of projects, 67-85
    funding for, 12-13, 123-124
    future of, 123-124
    lending hardware and software for, 63-64
    management of, 13, 51-55, 58-62
    online services, 115-118
    promotion of, 97-101
    purpose of, 4-5
    training for, 55-58
    user groups, 38, 90-91
        See also Electronic bulletin board system (BBS), Microcomputer, Software
Public Access Microcomputer Users Group (PAMUG), 90
Public Library Association Micro Task Force, 90

Radio Shack, 13
Resources in Computer Education (RICE), 42

Right On Programs, 47
Rockwell Gardens Reading and Study Center, 73
Rolling Meadows Library, 58, 80-81

Sager, Donald, 70
San Mateo County Office of Education, 44
Scarborough Systems, 48
Scholastic Inc., 48, 50
Scott Adams' Adventures, 85
Scottsdale Public Library, 81
Screenwriter, 34, 49, 79
Sherman Park Branch Library, 73, 97
Sherman, Ted, 67
Sierra On-Line Inc., 49
Sinclair ZX81, 4
Sirius Software, 50
Sir-Tech Software, Inc., 50
Small Computers in Libraries, 41
Softalk, 41
Softswap, 44, 49
Software
   defined, 29-30
   for public access, 47-50
   information sources, 41-42
   organizing a collection, 44-47
   selection of, 36-40
   types of, 7, 31-36
   vendors, 42-44
Software Review, 41
Software Vendor Directory, 42
Software Wall Chart, 45, 121
Soldier Creek Press, 45
Sorcim Corp., 50
The Source, 4, 5, 103, 115, 116, 117, 118
Southern Adirondack Library System, 84, 124
Speak N' Spell, 4, 18, 70
Spinnaker Software Corp., 47
Standard & Poor's News, 117
Startrek, 49
Station II: Apple Support System, 52
Story Machine, 49

Subject Guide Wall Chart, 119-121
SuperCalc, 34, 50
Superscribe, 34
Swift's Educational Software Directory, 22

Tandy Corp., 26
   TRS-80, 26, 27, 49, 52, 74, 104
TAVA Corp., 26-27
Tec-Mart Inc., 52
Telenet, 116
Tele-Terminals, 52
Texas Instruments, 25, 49
   TI 99/4A, 25, 75, 81
Three Mile Island, 50
Tic-Tac-Facts, 50
Timex-Sinclair, 19, 25, 75
Timex-Sinclair 1983 Directory, 25
TRS-80. *See* Tandy Corp.
TRW, Inc., 24
Tymnet, 116
Type Attack, 50
Typing Tutor II, 50

Ultima, 85
Ulysses and the Golden Fleece, 49, 79
Upper Arlington Public Library, 74

Valdez, 50
VisiCalc, 34, 50, 79, 80, 93

Wall chart. *See* Software Wall Chart, Subject Guide Wall Chart
Warner-Amex Qube, 75
Waukegan Public Library, 104, 111
Wilburn, Gene and Marion, 103
Wilmette Public Library, 84-85
Wisconsin Educational Media Association, 45
Wizardry, 50, 77
WordStar, 34, 50, 80
World Book Encyclopedia, 117

Zork I, II, III, 50

ABOUT THE AUTHOR

Patrick R. Dewey is branch librarian at the North-Pulaski Branch of the Chicago Public Library, and founder of its Personal Computer Center. He has been with the Chicago Public Library for nine years. Mr. Dewey has an active interest in microcomputers and their use with the public. He has written extensively on the subject for a number of professional journals, and is currently an assistant editor of *Software Review*. He received a B.A. in psychology from Oakland University and an M.L.S. from Wayne State University.